Piano · Vocal · Guitar

THE MOST REQUESTED
ISLAND SONGS

ISBN 978-1-4950-7573-5

cherry lane
music company

EXCLUSIVELY DISTRIBUTED BY

HAL•LEONARD®

7777 W. BLUEMOUND RD. P.O. BOX 13819 MILWAUKEE, WI 53213

Visit Hal Leonard Online at
www.halleonard.com

CONTENTS

ALOHA OE

Words and Music by
QUEEN LILIUOKALANI

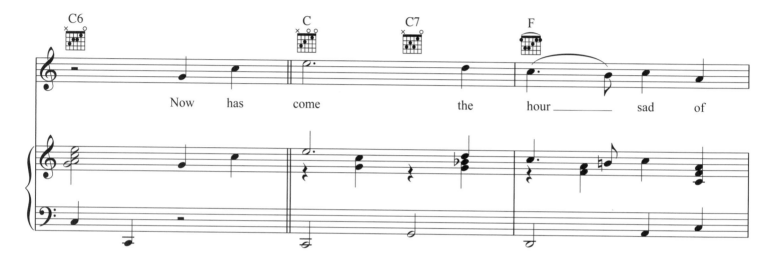

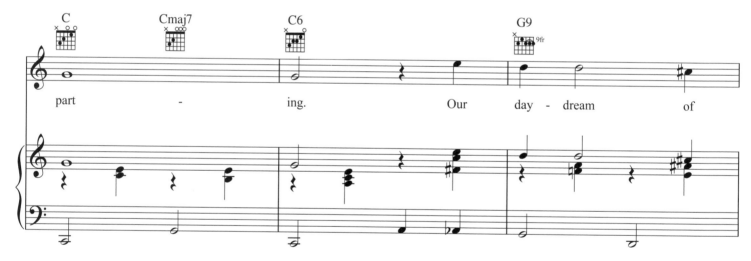

Now has come the hour _____ sad of part - ing. Our day - dream of

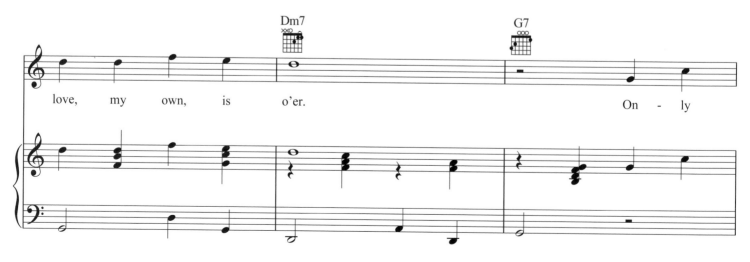

love, my own, is o'er. On - ly

mem - o - ries will soon be left

us; let our lives seem to glide on as be -

fore. Fare - well, dear

love, I'll dream of you. No

pass - ing grief is this my heart is feel -

ing. I love you so; be -

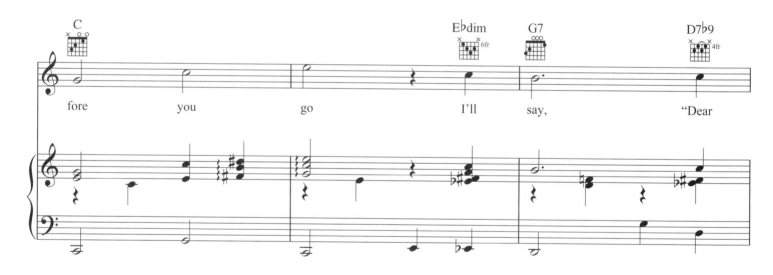

fore you go I'll say, "Dear

loved one, fare - well."

BALI HA'I

from SOUTH PACIFIC

Lyrics by OSCAR HAMMERSTEIN II
Music by RICHARD RODGERS

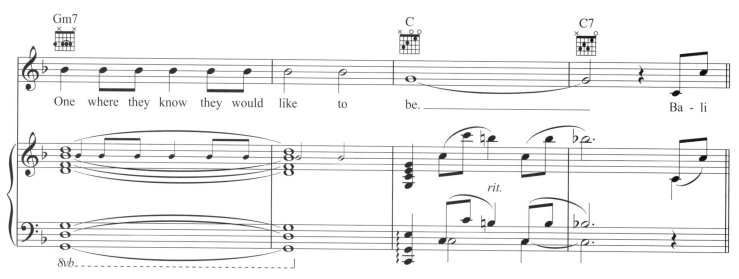

One where they know they would like to be. _____ Ba - li

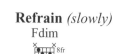

Refrain *(slowly)*

Ha'i may call you an - y night, An - y day. In your

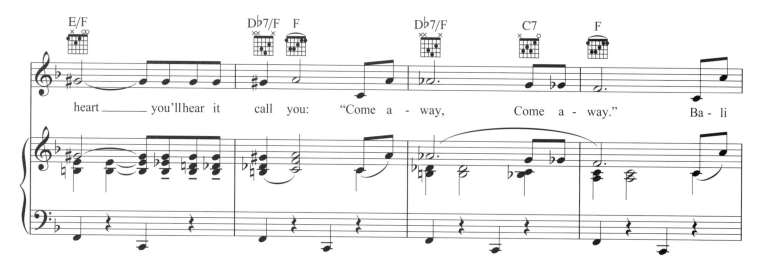

heart _____ you'll hear it call you: "Come a - way, Come a - way." Ba - li

Ha'i will whis - per On the wind of the sea: "Here am

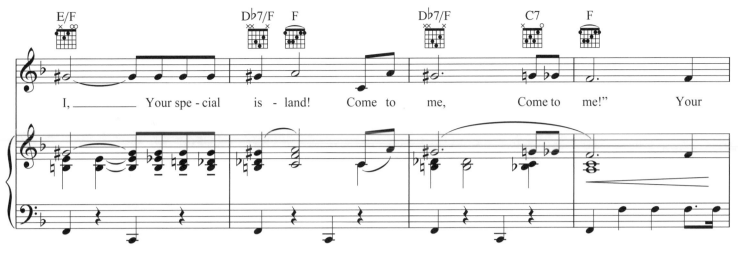

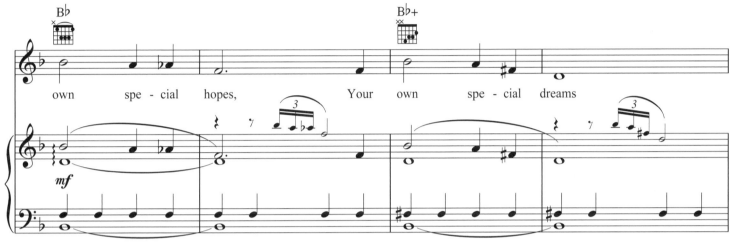

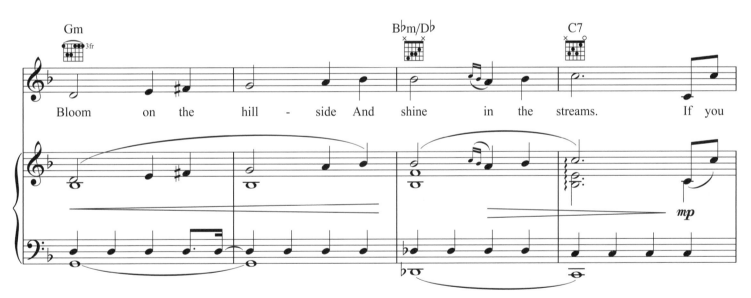

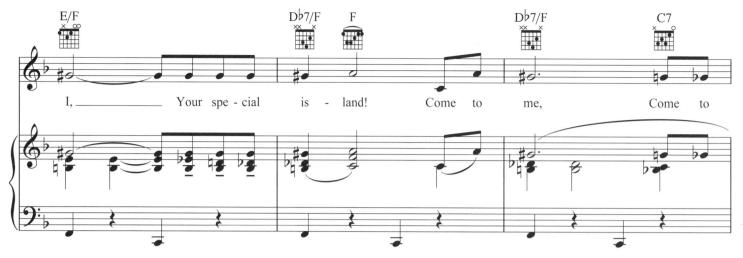

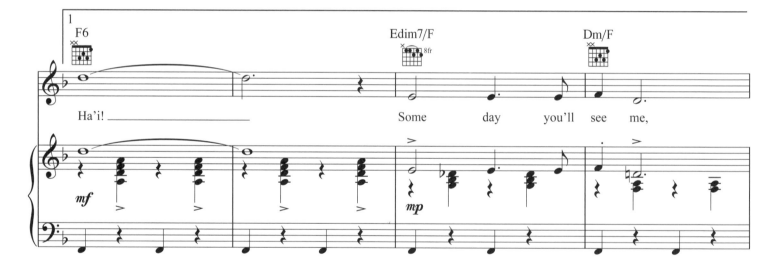

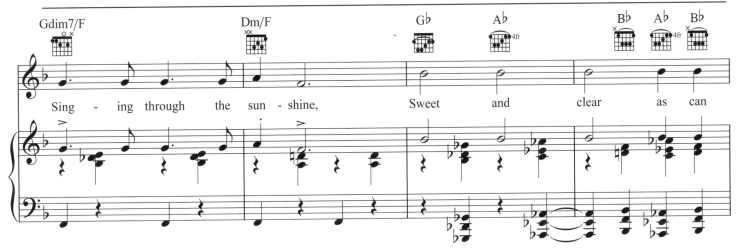

BEYOND THE RAINBOW

Words by LEON POBER
Music by WEBLEY EDWARDS

BEYOND THE SEA

Lyrics by JACK LAWRENCE
Music by CHARLES TRENET and ALBERT LASRY
Original French Lyric to "La Mer" by
CHARLES TRENET

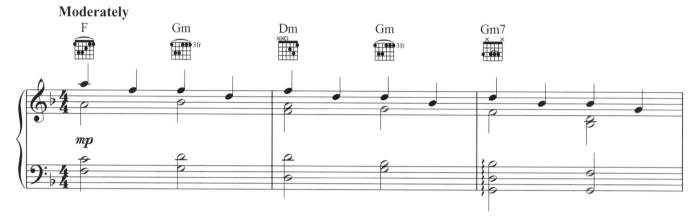

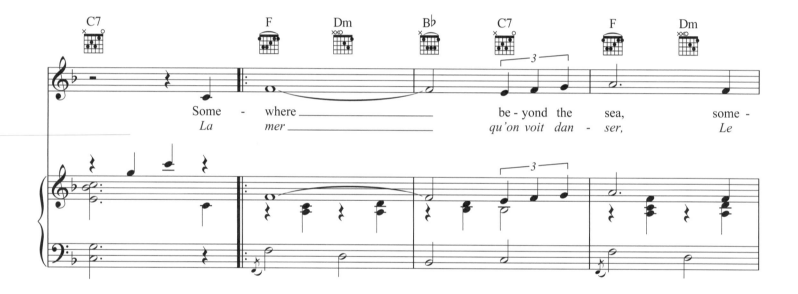

Some - where _____ be - yond the sea, some -
La mer _____ qu'on voit dan - ser, Le

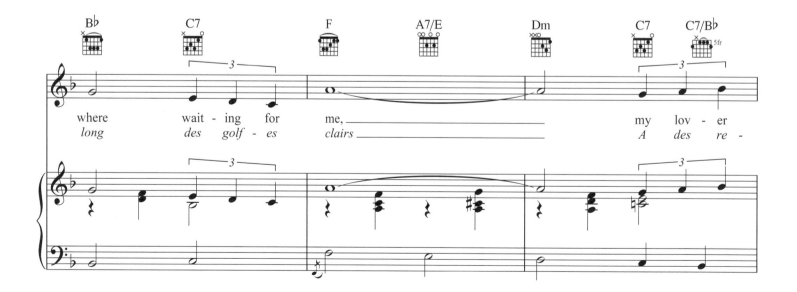

where wait - ing for me, _____ my lov - er
long des golf - es clairs _____ A des re -

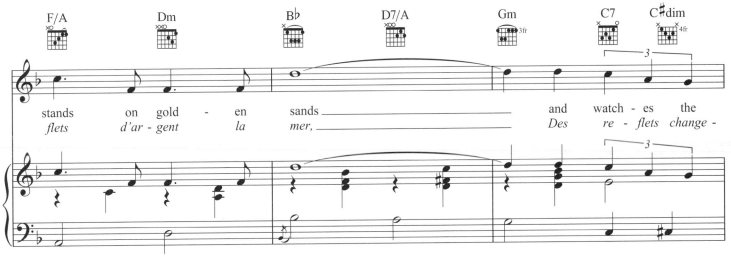

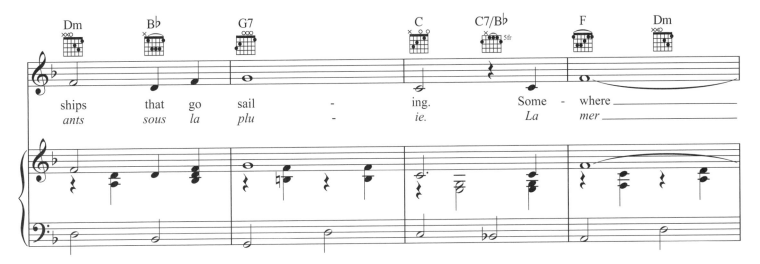

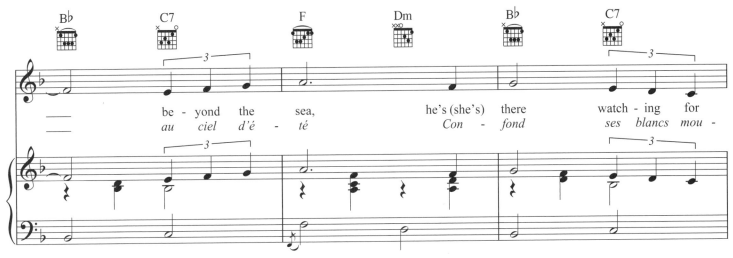

soon. _____ We'll meet _____ be - yond the
llées. _____ La mer _____ les a ber -

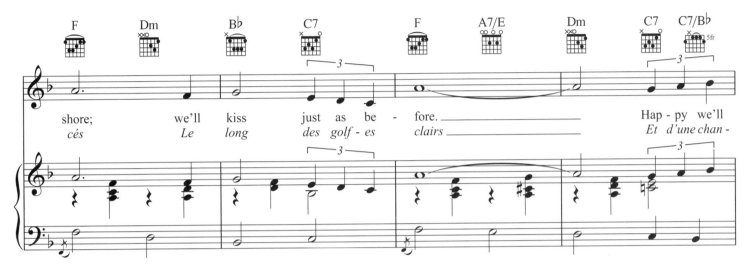

shore; we'll kiss just as be - fore. _____ Hap - py we'll
cés Le long des golf - es clairs _____ Et d'une chan -

be be - yond the sea, _____ and nev - er a - gain I'll go
son d'a mour, la mer _____ A ber - cé mon coeur pour la

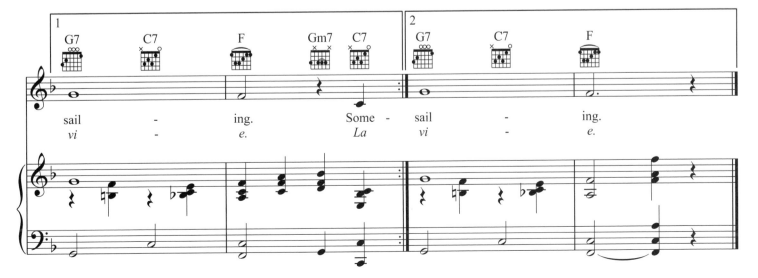

sail - ing. Some - sail - ing.
vi - e. La vi - e.

BLUE HAWAII

from the Paramount Picture WAIKIKI WEDDING

Words and Music by LEO ROBIN
and RALPH RAINGER

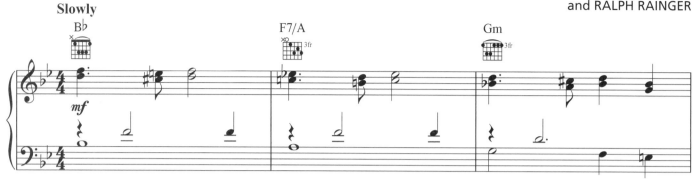

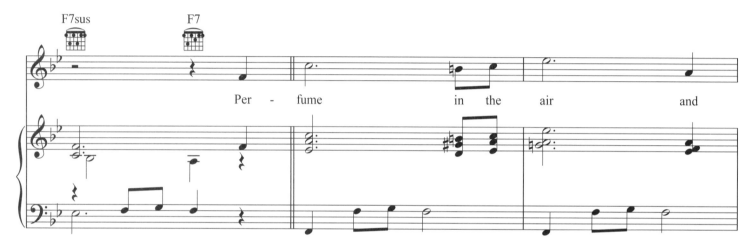

Per- fume in the air and

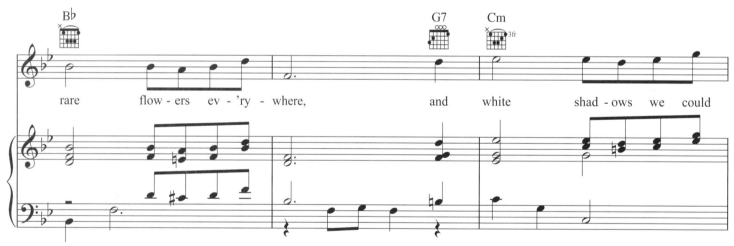

rare flow- ers ev - 'ry - where, and white shad - ows we could

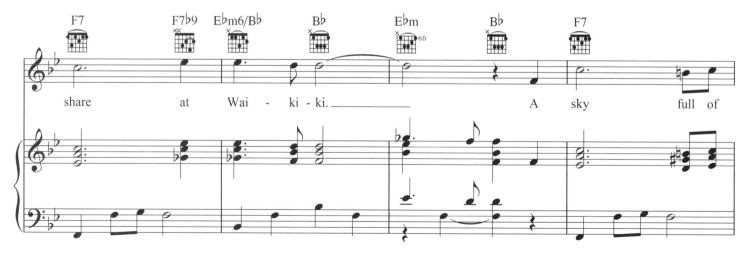

share at Wai - ki - ki. A sky full of

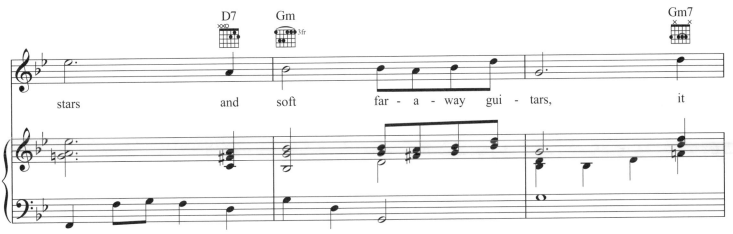

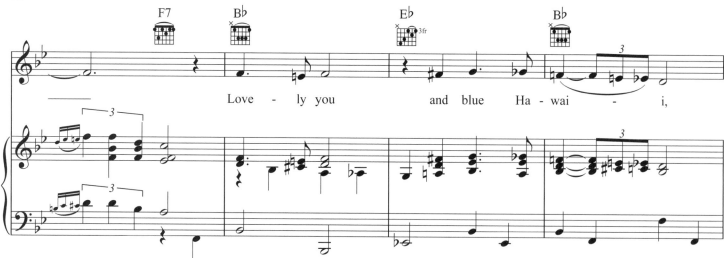

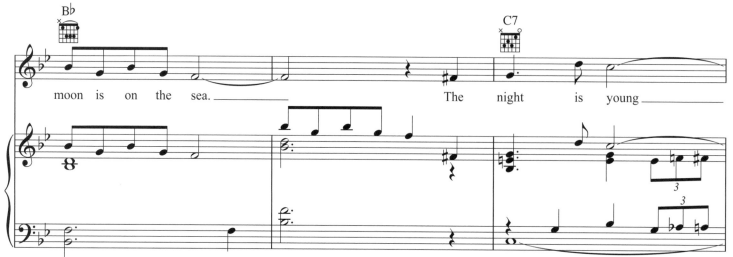

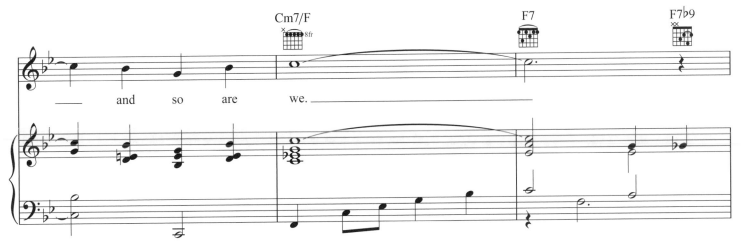

and so are we.

Dreams come true in blue Ha - wai - i

and mine could all come true this ___ mag - ic

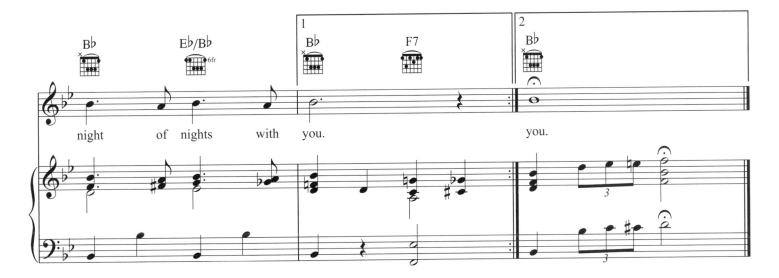

night of nights with you.   you.

BROWN EYED GIRL

Words and Music by
VAN MORRISON

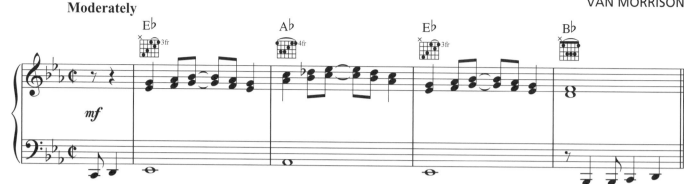

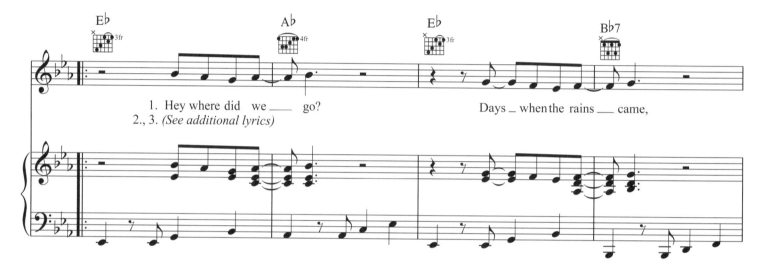

1. Hey where did we ___ go?
2., 3. (See additional lyrics)

Days ___ when the rains ___ came,

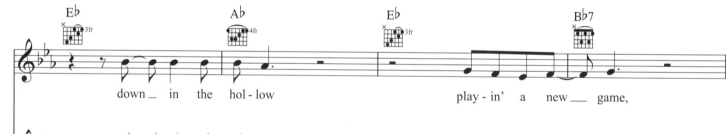

down ___ in the hol-low

play-in' a new ___ game,

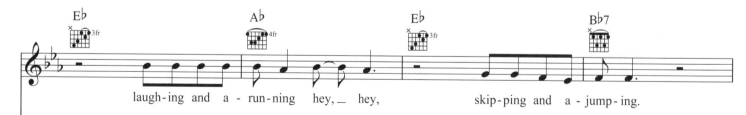

laugh-ing and a - run-ning hey, ___ hey,

skip-ping and a - jump-ing.

In the mist - y morn - ing fog ___ with our hearts a - thump - in', and

you, ___ my brown eyed girl. _____

You, my brown eyed girl. ___ Do you re-mem -

Chorus

- ber when we used to sing: ___ sha la __ la la __

Additional Lyrics

2. Whatever happened to Tuesday and so slow
   Going down the old mine with a transistor radio
   Standing in the sunlight laughing
   Hiding behind a rainbow's wall
   Slipping and a-sliding
   All along the waterfall
   With you, my brown eyed girl
   You, my brown eyed girl.
   Do you remember when we used to sing:
   Chorus

3. So hard to find my way, now that I'm all on my own
   I saw you just the other day, my, how you have grown
   Cast my memory back there, Lord
   Sometime I'm overcome thinking 'bout
   Making love in the green grass
   Behind the stadium
   With you, my brown eyed girl
   With you, my brown eyed girl.
   Do you remember when we used to sing:
   Chorus

COME MONDAY

Words and Music by
JIMMY BUFFETT

And, hon - ey, I did - n't know _ that I'd be miss -
And, dar - lin', it's I love you so, ___ that's the rea - son I just _
Cal - i - for - nia has worn me quite thin; _ I just can't wait to see _

- in' you so. ___
___ let you go. } Come Mon - day _ it - 'll be all right. _ Come
___ you a - gain.

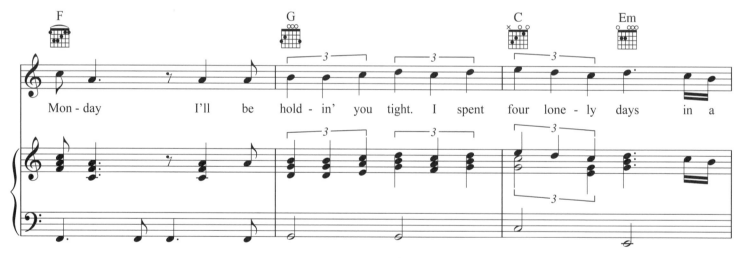

Mon - day I'll be hold - in' you tight. I spent four lone - ly days in a

brown L. A. haze _ and I just want you back by my side.

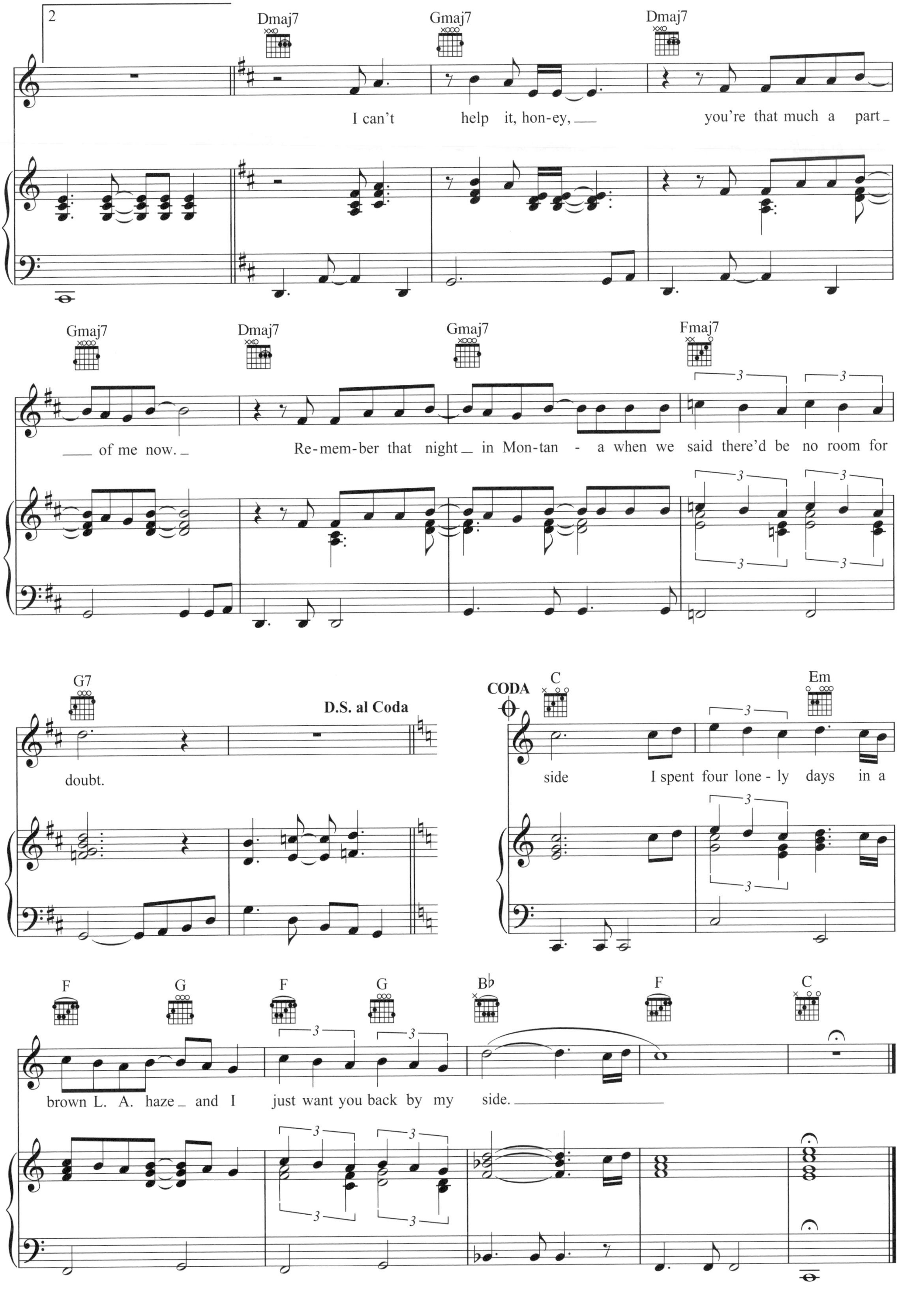
2
Dmaj7
Gmaj7
Dmaj7
I can't help it, hon-ey, you're that much a part
Gmaj7
Dmaj7
Gmaj7
Fmaj7
of me now. Re-mem-ber that night in Mon-tan - a when we said there'd be no room for
G7
D.S. al Coda
doubt.
CODA
C
Em
side I spent four lone - ly days in a
F
G
F
G
B♭
F
C
brown L. A. haze and I just want you back by my side.

COCONUT

Words and Music by
HARRY NILSSON

lime in the co-co-nut, drink 'em both to-geth-er, put the lime in the co-co-nut, then _
lime in the co-co-nut, drink 'em both up, put the lime in the co-co-nut,

To Coda ⊕

_ you feel bet - ter. Put the lime in the co - co - nut, drink 'em both up. Put the
drink 'em both up. Put the lime in the co - co - nut, drink 'em both up. Put the

lime in the co - co - nut, call me in the morn - ing. Oo, _____ oo, _____

1.

2.

D.S. al Coda

_ oo, _____ oo, _____ oo, _____ oo. _____ oo. _____

CODA

lime in the co-co-nut. You're such a sil-ly crab. Put the lime in the co-co-nut,

drink 'em both to-geth-er, put the lime in the co-co-nut, then ___ you feel ___ bet-ter. Put the

lime in the co-co-nut, drink 'em both up. Put the lime in the co-co-nut,

Repeat and Fade

call me in the morn - ing.
Yes, if you call me in the morn-ing, I'll tell ___ you what to do. Yes, if you

COULD YOU BE LOVED

Words and Music by
BOB MARLEY

Moderately bright Reggae

Could you be loved ____

and be loved? _____

Don't let them fool you
Don't let them change you

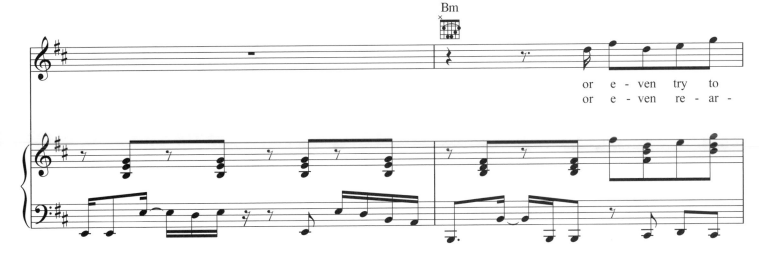

or e - ven try to
or e - ven re - ar -

school you,
range you,
oh, no.
oh, no.

We've got a mind of our own. So, go to
We've got a life to ___ live.

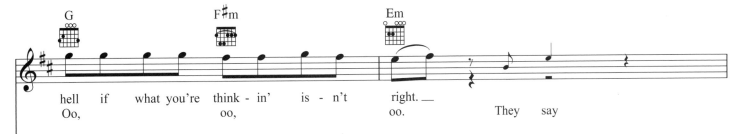

hell if what you're think - in' is - n't right. ___
Oo, oo, oo. They say

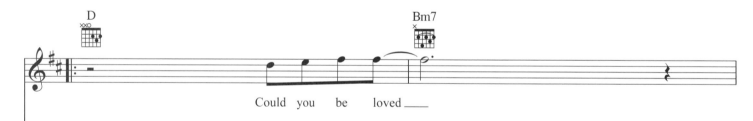

The

road of life is rock - y and you may stum - ble too. __ So

while you point your fin - gers, some - one else is judg - in' you. Love __

__ your broth - er man. __
Could you be, could you be, could you be loved? Could you be, could you be loved? __

Could you be, could you be, could you be loved? Could you be, could you be loved?

CODA

Stay a - live __ oh. Could you be loved __

Bm

G

and be loved? __

1 D

2 D

You

ain't gon-na miss your wa - ter un - til your well __ runs dry. __ No

mat - ter how __ you treat __ him, the man will nev - er be sat - is - fied.

Could you be, could you be, could you be loved? Could you be, could you be loved?

Repeat and Fade

Say some - thin', say some - thin'.

DAY-O
(The Banana Boat Song)

Words and Music by IRVING BURGIE
and WILLIAM ATTAWAY

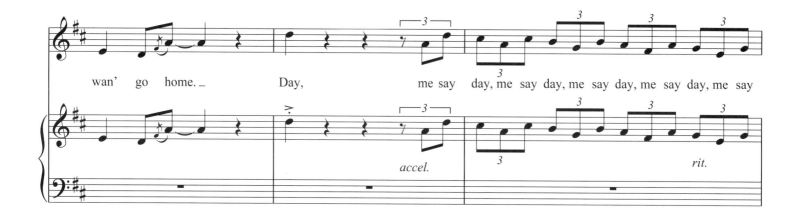

Moderate Calypso

Work all night _ on a drink of rum. _ Day - light come _ and me

wan' go home. Stack ba - nan - a till de morn - ing come. _

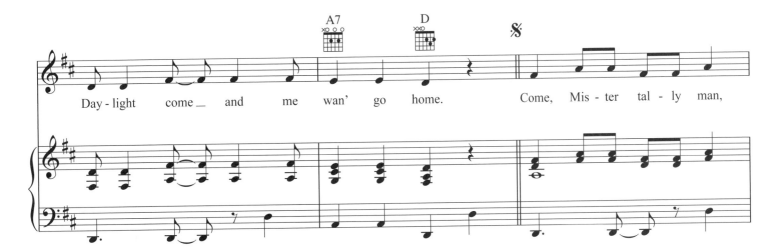

Day - light come _ and me wan' go home. Come, Mis - ter tal - ly man,

tal - ly me ba - nan - a. Day - light come _ and me wan' go home.

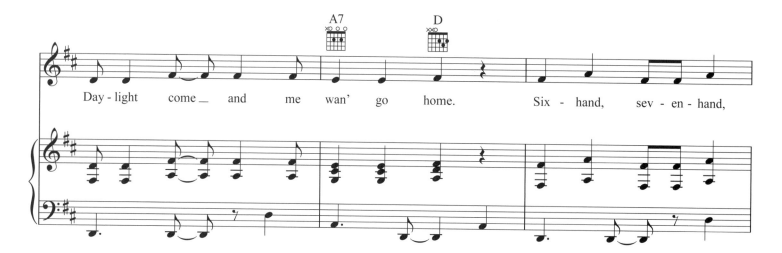

Day, me say day - o. ___ Day - light come ___ and me

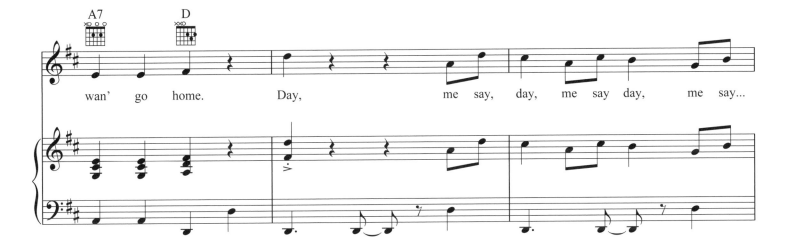

wan' go home. Day, me say, day, me say day, me say...

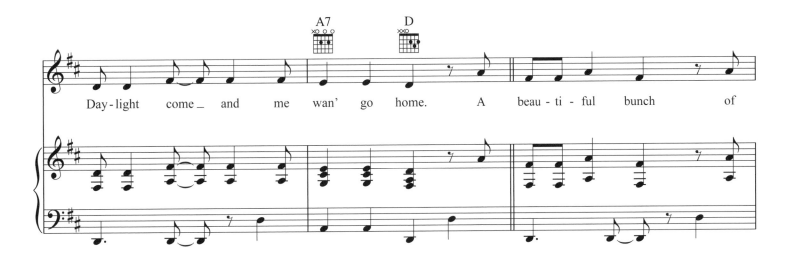

Day - light come ___ and me wan' go home. A beau - ti - ful bunch of

ripe ba - nan - a. Day - light come ___ and me wan' go home.

Hide the dead - ly black ta - ran - t'la. Day - light come _ and me

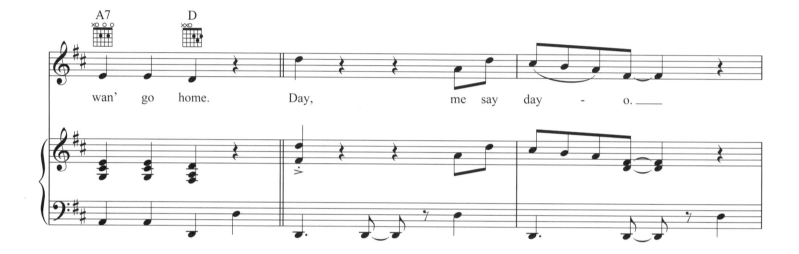

wan' go home. Day, me say day - o. ___

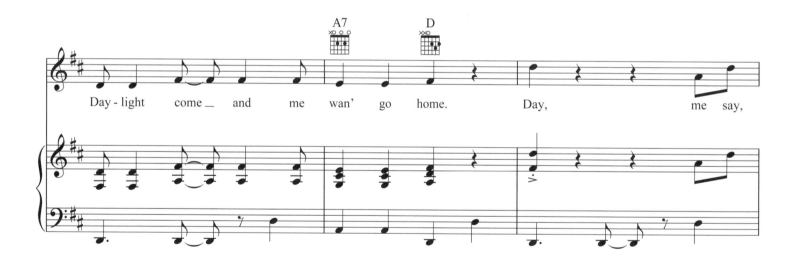

Day - light come _ and me wan' go home. Day, me say,

day, me say day, me say... Day - light come _ and me wan' go home.

D.S. al Coda

DON'T WORRY, BE HAPPY

Words and Music by
BOBBY McFERRIN

Brightly

(Whistle, add higher notes on repeat)

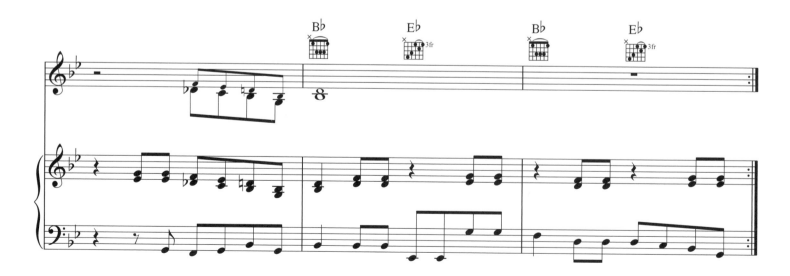

Spoken ad lib. over Repeat and Fade:

Don't worry. Don't worry. Don't do it.
Be Happy. Put a smile on your face.
Don't bring everybody down. Don't worry.
It will soon pass, whatever it is.
Don't worry. Be happy. I'm not worried.
I'm happy.

DOWN UNDER

Words and Music by COLIN HAY
and RON STRYKERT

Steady 4, with a Ska feel

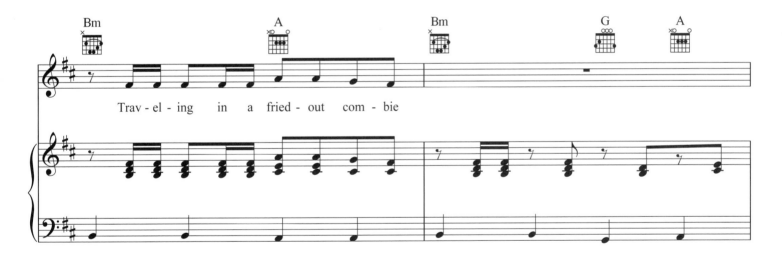

Trav-el-ing in a fried-out com-bie

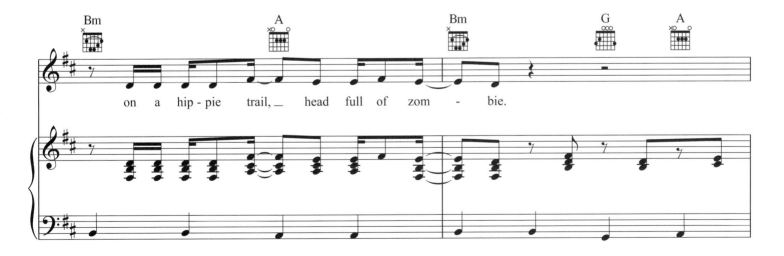

on a hip-pie trail, __ head full of zom - bie.

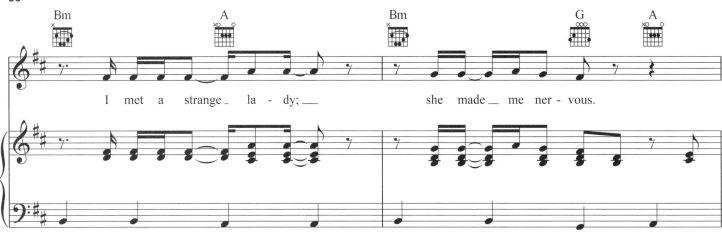

I met a strange __ la - dy; ___ she made __ me ner - vous.

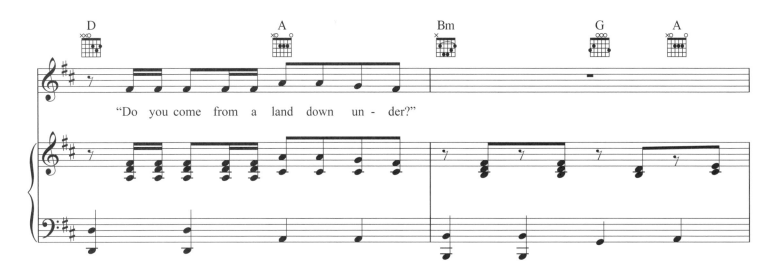

She took me in ___ and gave me break - fast. And she said,

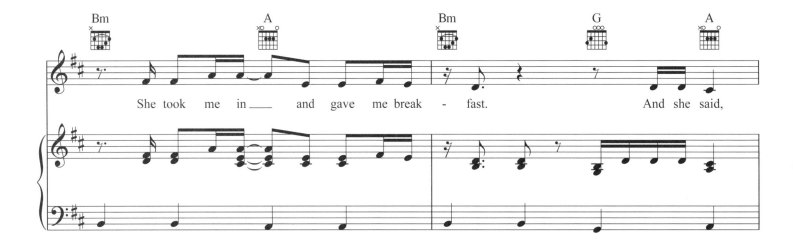

"Do you come from a land down un - der?"

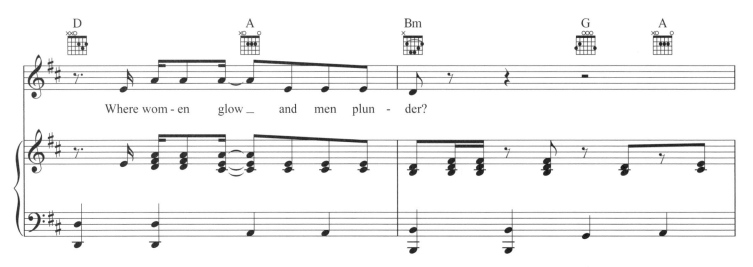

Where wom - en glow __ and men plun - der?

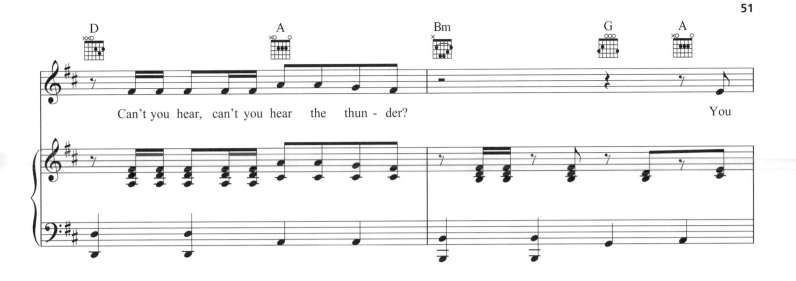

Can't you hear, can't you hear the thun - der? You

bet - ter run, __ you bet - ter take __ cov - er." __

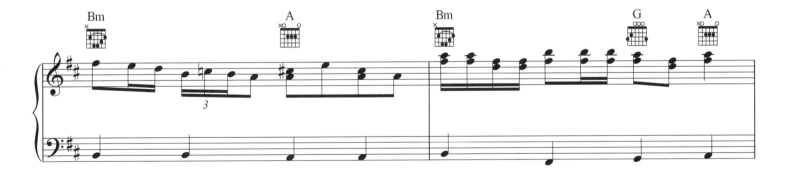

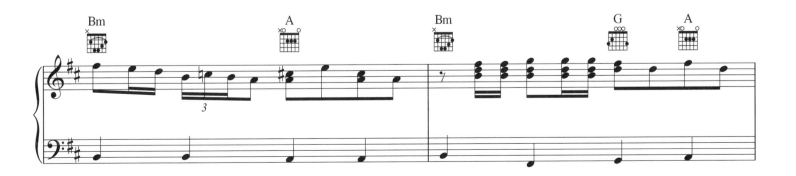

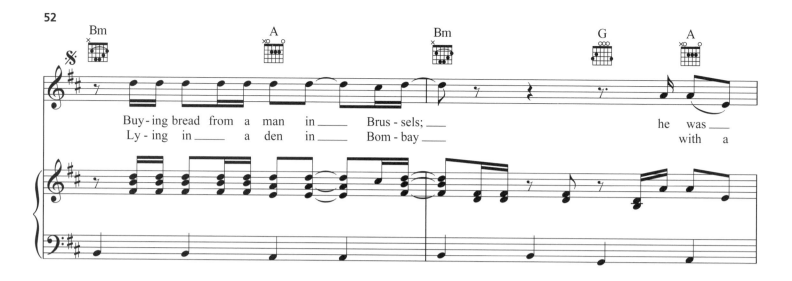

Buy - ing bread from a man in ___ Brus - sels; ___ he was ___
Ly - ing in ___ a den in ___ Bom - bay ___ with a

six - foot four and full of mus - cles.
slack jaw and not much to ___ say.

I said, "Do you speak - a my lan - guage?" ___
I said to the man, "Are you try'n to tempt me

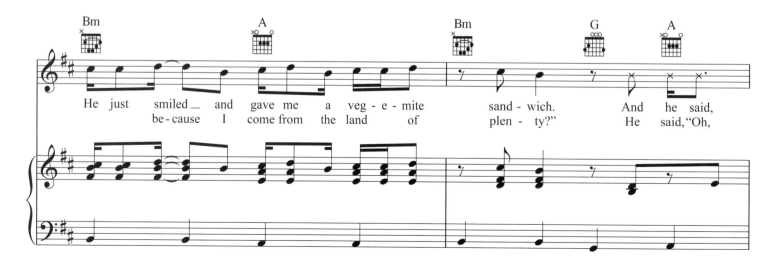

He just smiled ___ and gave me a veg - e - mite sand - wich. And he said,
be - cause I come from the land of plen - ty?" He said, "Oh,

"I come from a land down un - der _____
do you come from a land down un - der _____

where beer does flow __ and men chun - der. }
where wom - en glow __ and men plun - der? }

Can't you hear, can't you hear the thun - der? _____ You

To Coda ⊕

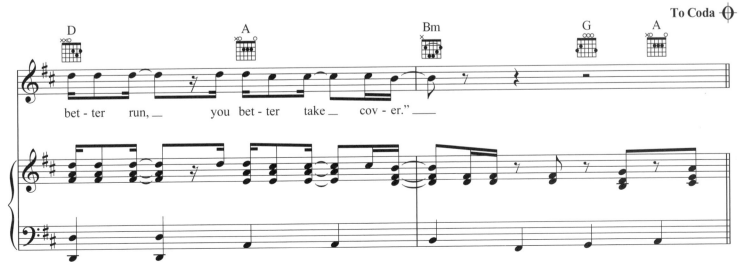

bet - ter run, __ you bet - ter take __ cov - er." _____

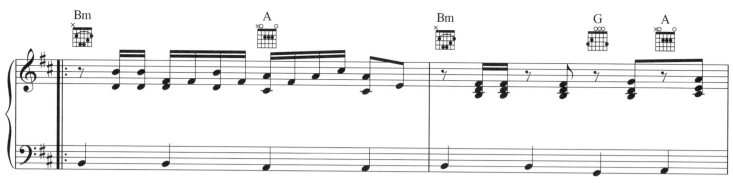

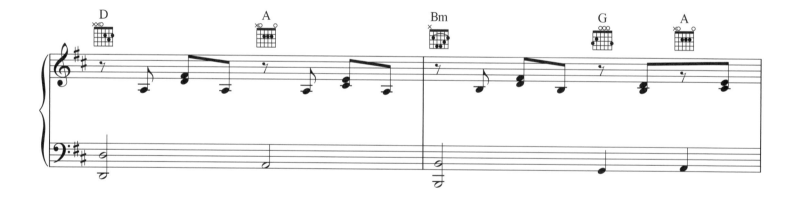

D.S. al Coda

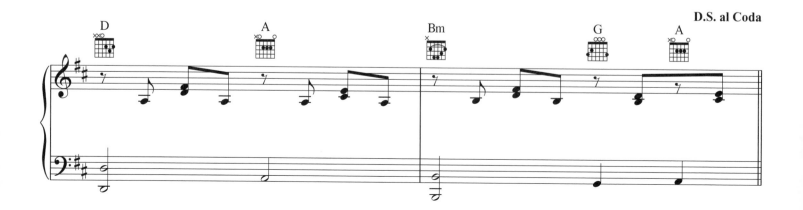

"Do you come from a land down un - der?

Where wom - en glow __ and men plun - der?

Can't you hear, can't you hear the thun - der? You

Repeat and Fade

bet - ter run, __ you bet - ter take __ cov - er." __

DRIFTING AND DREAMING
(Sweet Paradise)

Words by HAVEN GILLESPIE
Music by EGBERT VAN ALSTYNE,
ERWIN R. SCHMIDT and LOYAL CURTIS

call. _____ Love's old sweet sto -

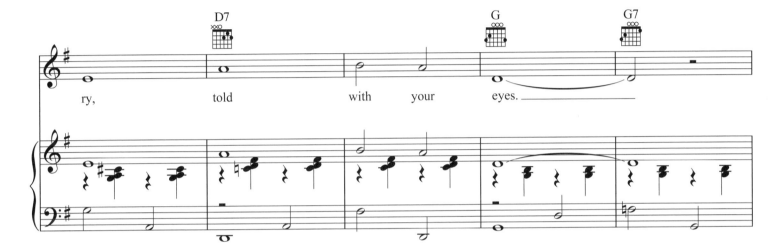

ry, told with your eyes. _____

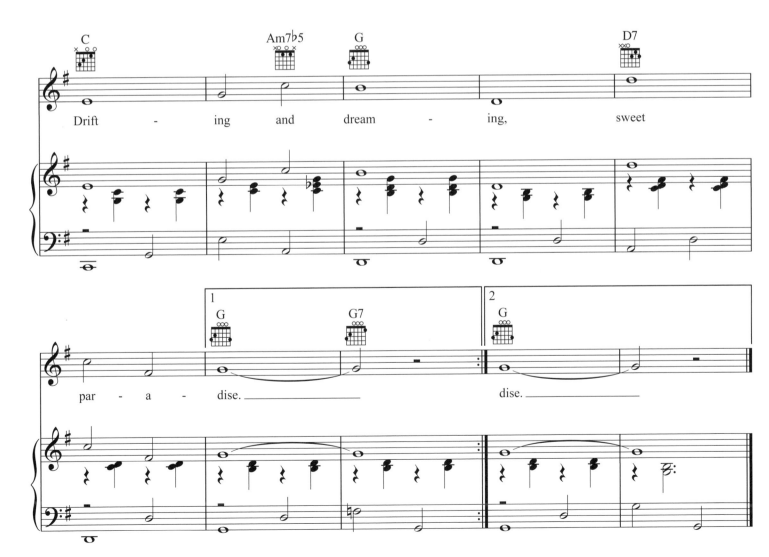

Drift - ing and dream - ing, sweet

par - a - dise. _____ dise. _____

ELECTRIC AVENUE

Words and Music by
EDDY GRANT

Who is to blame in what coun - try? Nev - er can get to the one.

Deal-ing in mul - ti - pli - ca - tion and they still can't feed ev - 'ry - one.

Oh, no, we're gon - na rock down to E - lec - tric Av - e - nue and

then we'll take it high - er. Oh, we gon - na rock down to E - lec -

ESCAPE
(The Piña Colada Song)

Words and Music by
RUPERT HOLMES

Moderate groove

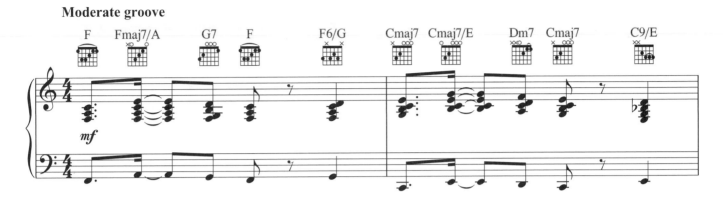

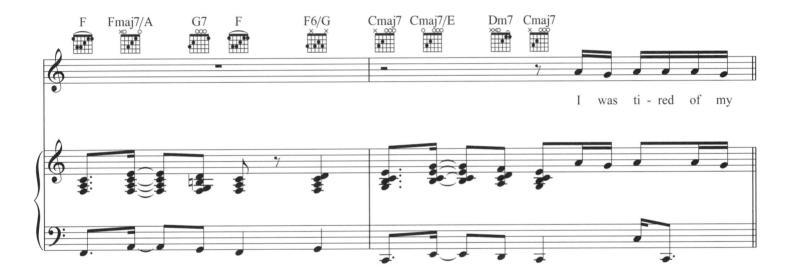

I was ti-red of my

la - dy,   we'd been to-geth-er too long. ___

la - dy,   I know I sound kind of mean. ___

hopes   and she walked in - to the place. ___

Like a worn-out re-cord-

But me and my old la -

I knew her smile in an in-

- ing .... of my fa-vor-ite song. ___ So while she lay .... there
- dy .... have fall-en in-to the same ___ old dull ___ rou-tine. ___ So I wrote to the
- stant, I knew the curve of her face. ___ It was my own love-ly

sleep-ing .... I read the pa-per in bed. ___ And in the per-son-al col-
pa-per, took out a per-son-al ad. ___ And though I'm no-bod-y's po-
la-dy, and she said, "Oh, it's you." ___ Then we laughed for a mo-

- umns, there was this let-ter I read: ___ If you like pi-ña co-
- et, I thought it was-n't half bad. ___ Yes, I like pi-ña co-
- ment, and I said, "I nev-er knew ___ that you liked pi-ña co-

la - das · and get-ting caught in the rain,
la - das · and get-ting caught in the rain.
la - das, · get-ting caught in the rain,

if you're not in - to
I'm not much in - to
and the feel of the

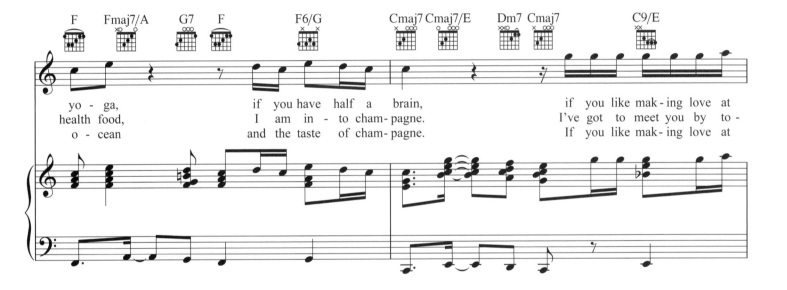

yo - ga, · if you have half a brain,
health food, · I am in - to cham-pagne.
o - cean · and the taste of cham-pagne.

if you like mak-ing love at
I've got to meet you by to-
If you like mak-ing love at

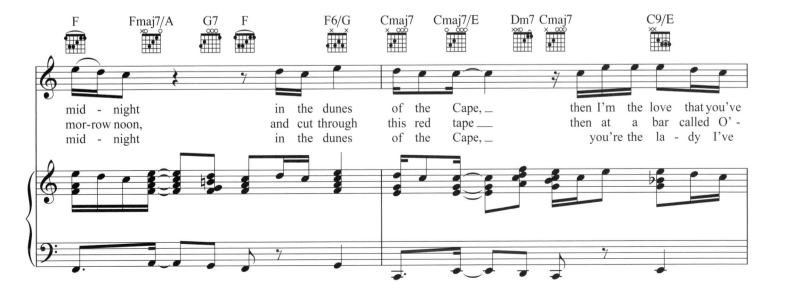

mid - night · in the dunes of the Cape, __
mor-row noon, · and cut through this red tape __
mid - night · in the dunes of the Cape, __

then I'm the love that you've
then at a bar called O'-
you're the la - dy I've

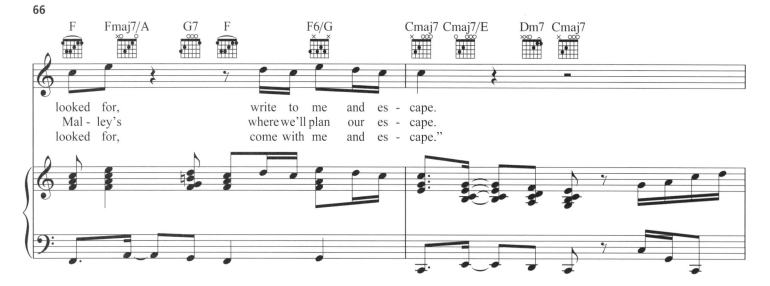

looked for,   write to me and es - cape.
Mal - ley's   where we'll plan our es - cape.
looked for,   come with me and es - cape."

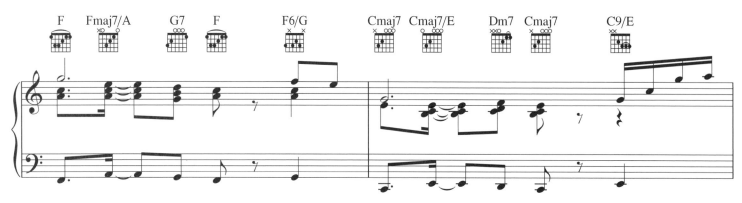

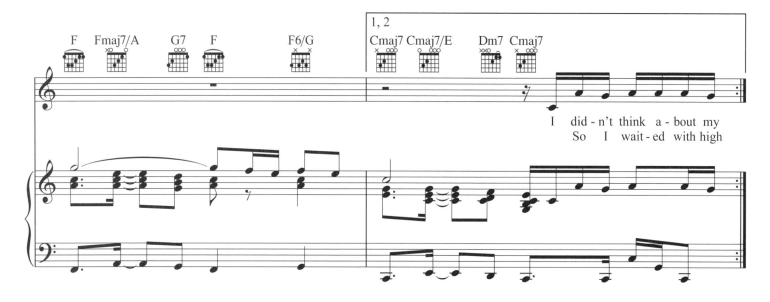

I did - n't think a - bout my
So   I   wait - ed with high

If you like pi - ña co - la - das   and get-ting caught in the

FAR AWAY PLACES

Words and Music by ALEX KRAMER
and JOAN WHITNEY

Far a-way plac-es with strange sound-in' names, far a-way o-ver the sea. Those far a-way plac-es with the strange sound-in' names are call-in',

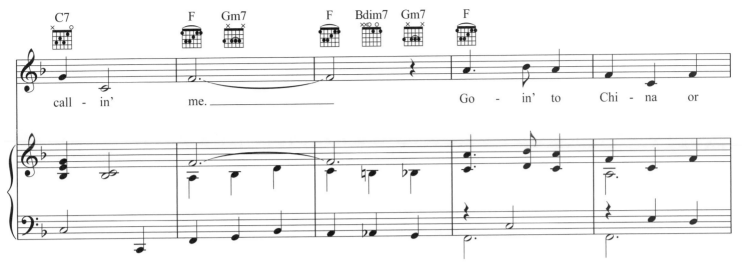

call - in' me. _____ Go - in' to Chi - na or

may - be Si - am, I wan - na see for my -

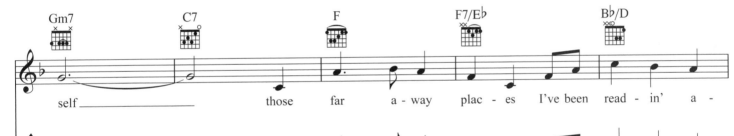

self _____ those far a - way plac - es I've been read - in' a -

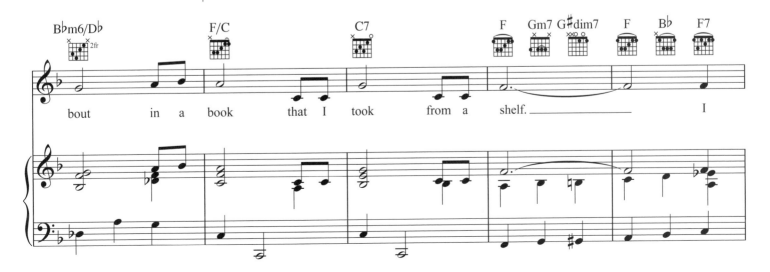

bout in a book that I took from a shelf. _____ I

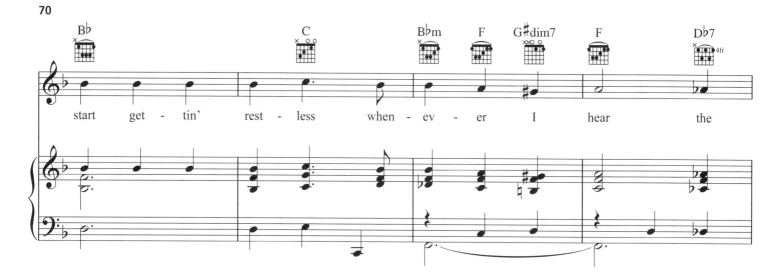

start get - tin' rest - less when - ev - er I hear the

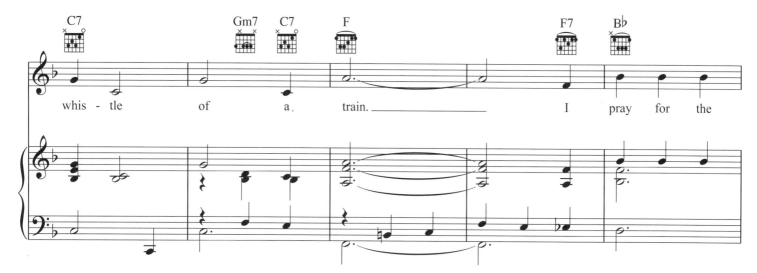

whis - tle of a train. _____ I pray for the

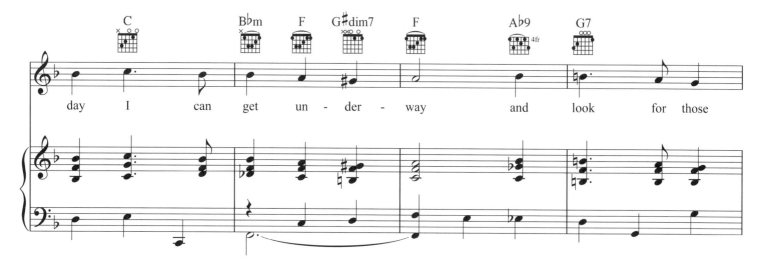

day I can get un - der - way and look for those

cas - tles in Spain. _____ They call me a dream - er, well,

GRAPEFRUIT-JUICY FRUIT

Words and Music by
JIMMY BUFFETT

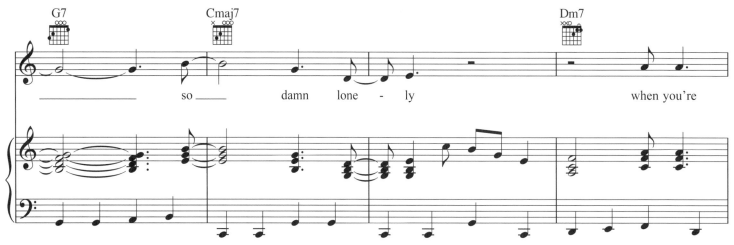

so ____ damn lone - ly   when you're

on   a plane a - lone.   *Solo ends*   Yes, and   if   I   had   the

And   if   I   had   that

mon-ey, hon - ey, I'd strap you in be-side ____ me,   and nev-er ev-er

leave   you,   leave you at ____ home all a - lone and cry - in'.

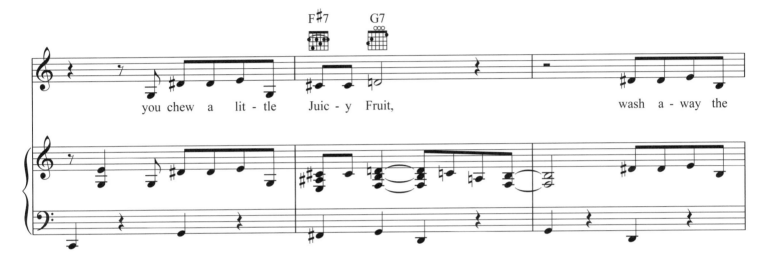

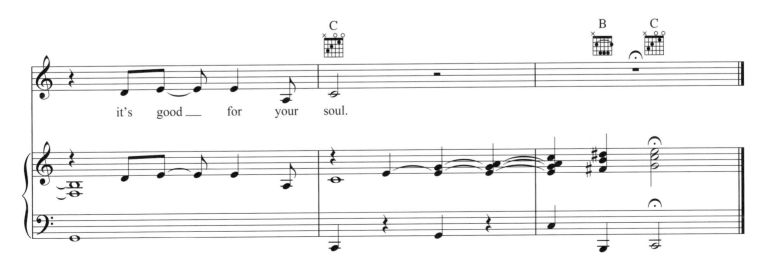

HARBOR LIGHTS

Words and Music by JIMMY KENNEDY
and HUGH WILLIAMS

har - bor lights. How could I help if tears were start - ing?

Good - bye to ten - der nights be - side the sil - v'ry

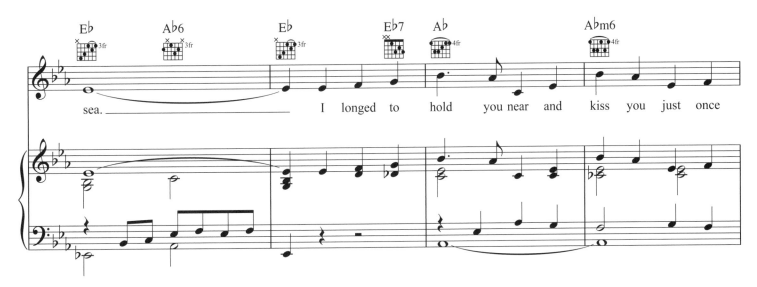

sea. _____ I longed to hold you near and kiss you just once

more, _____ but you were on the ship and I was on the

IN THE SUMMERTIME

Words and Music by
RAY DORSET

With a steady beat

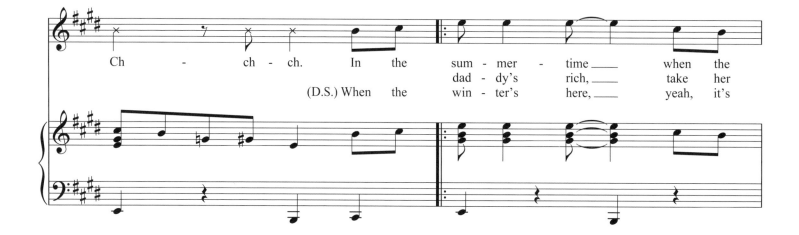

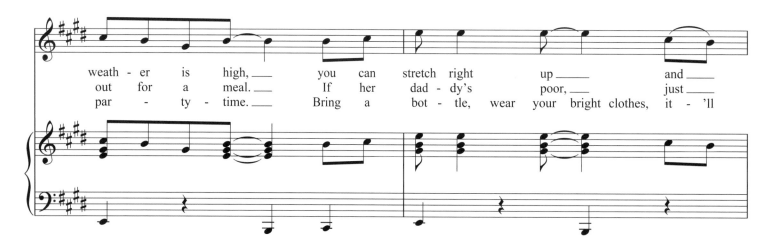

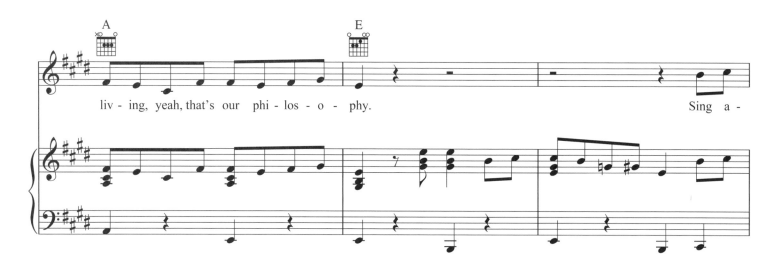

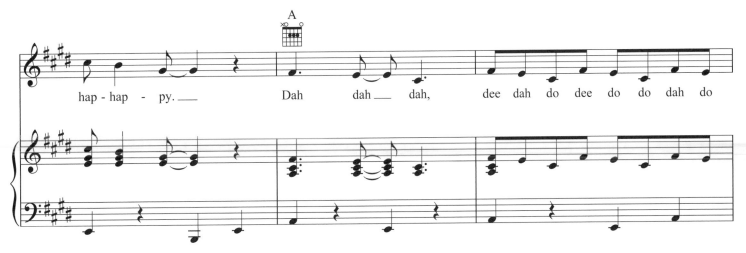

I CAN SEE CLEARLY NOW

Words and Music by
JOHNNY NASH

(Verse 1) I can see clear-ly now, the rain has gone.

(Verse 2) I think I can make it now, the pain has gone.

I can see all ob-sta-cles

All of the bad feel-ings have

in my way.

dis-ap-peared.

Gone are the dark

Here is that rain-

_____ clouds _____ that had _____ me blind. _____
- bow I've _____ been pray - ing for. _____

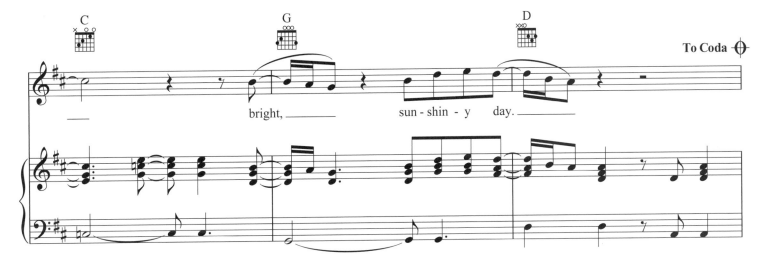

bright, _____ sun - shin - y day. _____

To Coda ⊕

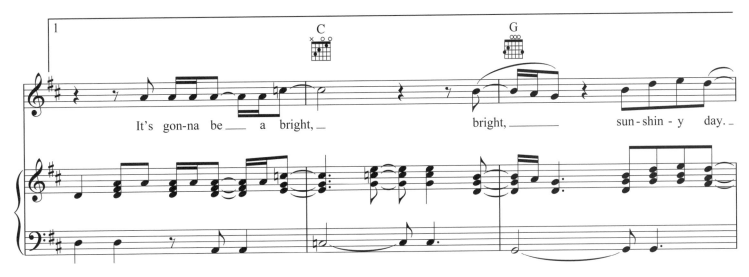

It's gon-na be _____ a bright, _____

bright, _____ sun - shin - y day. _____

Look all a - round, _____ there's noth - ing but blue skies. _____

_____ Look straight a - head, ___ noth - ing but

blue skies. _____

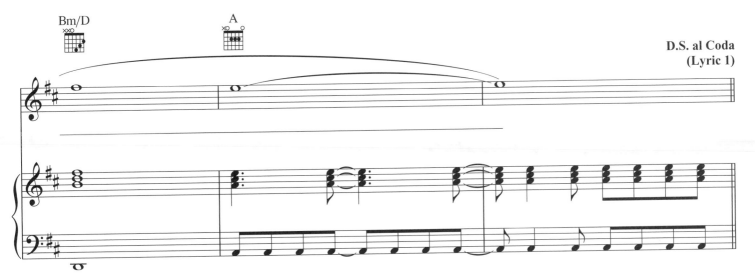

D.S. al Coda
(Lyric 1)

It's gon-na be ___ a bright, ___ bright, ___

___ sun-shin-y day. ___ It's gon-na be ___ a bright, ___

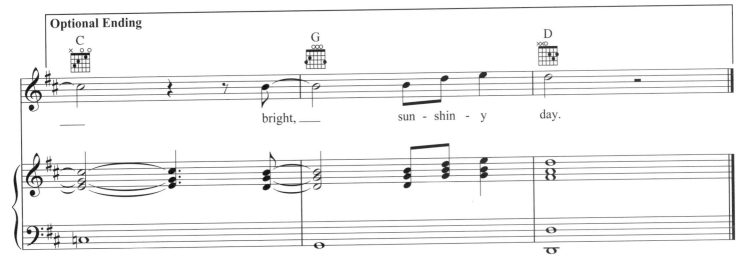

bright, ___ sun-shin-y day.

IS THIS LOVE

Words and Music by
BOB MARLEY

I wan-na love you and treat you right.____ I wan-na love

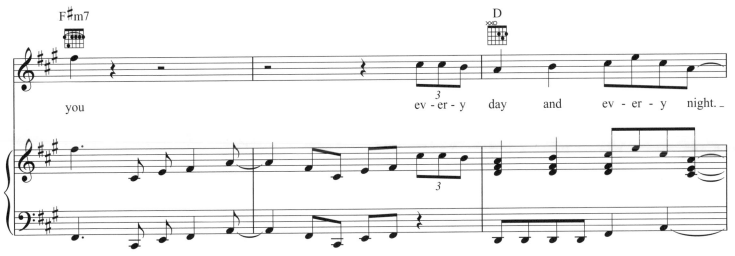

you

ev - er - y day and ev - er - y night. _

_ We'll be to - geth - er

with a

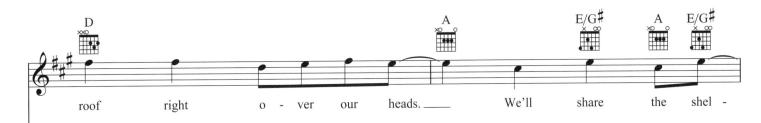

roof right o - ver our heads. _ We'll share the shel -

- ter

of my sin - gle bed. _

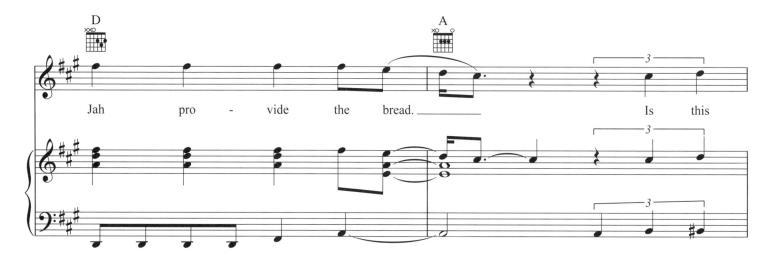

love, is this love, is this love, is this love that I'm

feel - in'?

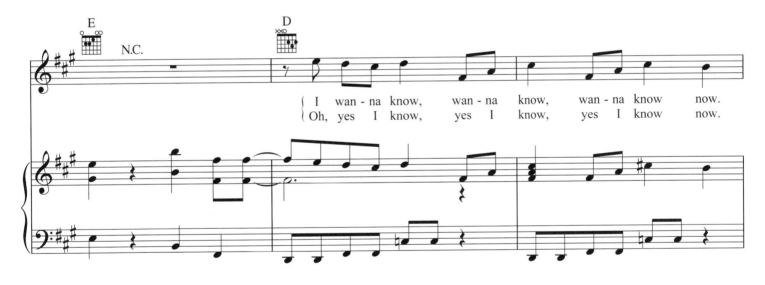

{ I wan - na know, wan - na know, wan - na know now.
{ Oh, yes I know, yes I know, yes I know now.

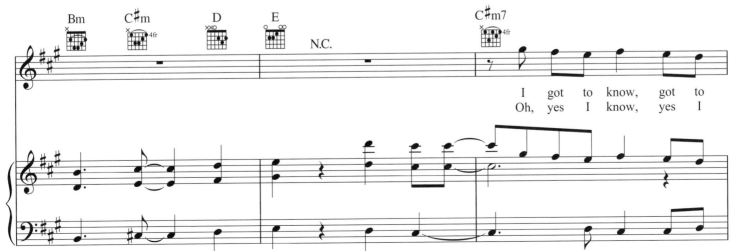

I got to know, got to
Oh, yes I know, yes I

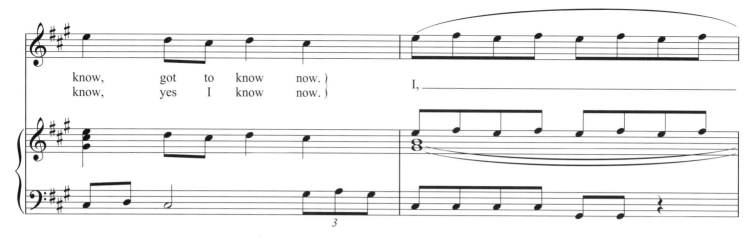

know, got to know now.
know, yes I know now.

I, _____

_____ I'm will - ing and a - ble,

so I throw my cards on your ta -

ble. I wan - na love See, I wan - na love

D.S. and Fade

JAMAICA FAREWELL

Words and Music by
IRVING BURGIE

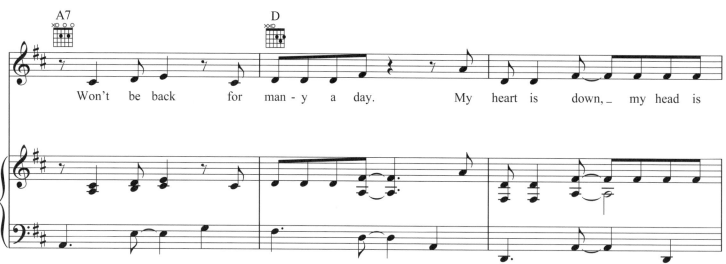

Won't be back for man-y a day. My heart is down,_ my head is

turn-ing a - round,_ I had to leave a lit - tle girl in King - ston town._

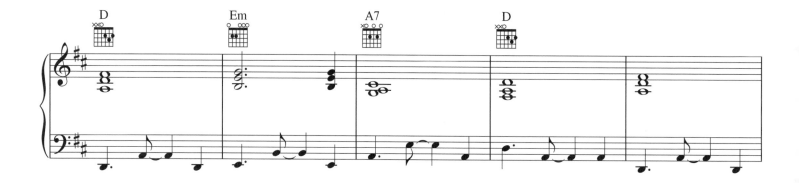

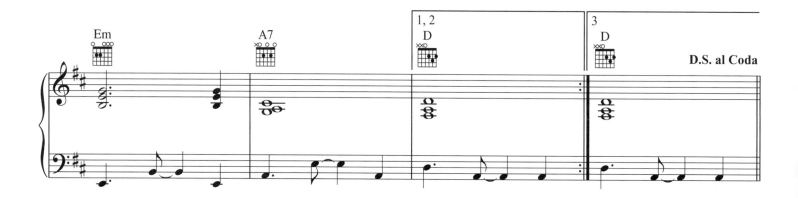

D.S. al Coda

CODA

Sad to say I'm on my way. _ Won't be back for man-y a day. My

heart is down, _ my head is turn ing a - round, _ I had to leave a lit - tle girl in King-ston town. _ My

Additional Lyrics

3. Down at the market you can hear
   Ladies cry out while on their heads they bear
   Ackie, rice; salt fish are nice,
   And the rum is fine any time of year.
   Chorus

ISLAND GIRL

Words and Music by ELTON JOHN
and BERNIE TAUPIN

Oh, _____ she's a big _____ girl, she's stand-ing six foot _____ three, _____

_____ turn-ing tricks for the dudes _____ in the

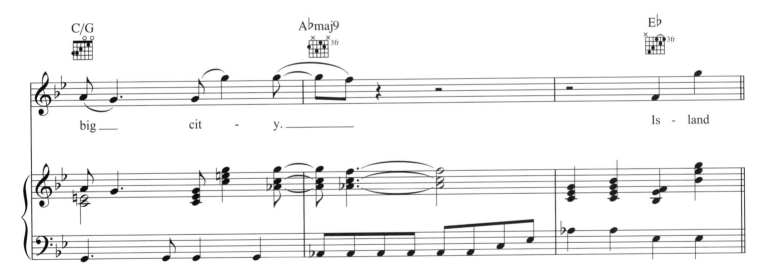

big _____ cit - y. _____ Is - land

girl, what you want - in' wid de white man's world? _____

Is - land girl, black boy want ___ you in his is - land world. ___

___ He want to take you from de

rack - et boss. ___ He want to save you, ___ but de cause ___ is lost.

Is - land girl, ___ is - land girl, ___ is - land girl, ___

tell ___ me what you want-in' wid de white man's ___ world. ___

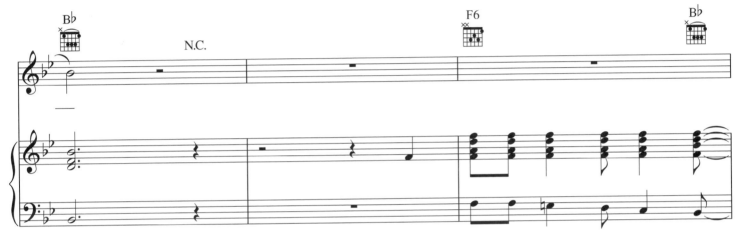

Well, she's *Instrumental*

black as coal, ___ but she burn ___ like a fire, ___

and she wrap ___ her-self a-round you   like a well-worn   tire. ___

___ You feel her nail   scratch ___ your ___ back ___

___ just like ___ a   rake. ___   Oh, _____ he

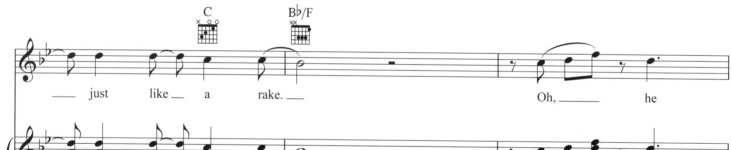

one more   gone, ___   he one ___ more   john ___   who make ___ de mis - take. ___

Instrumental ends

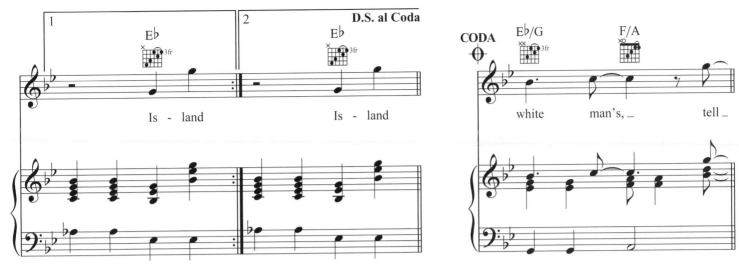

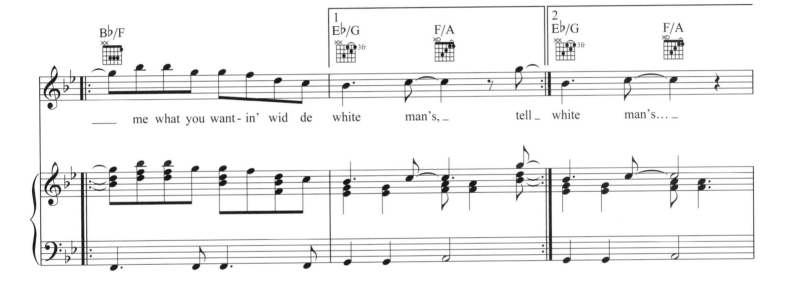

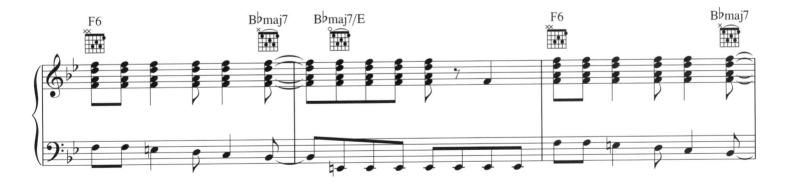

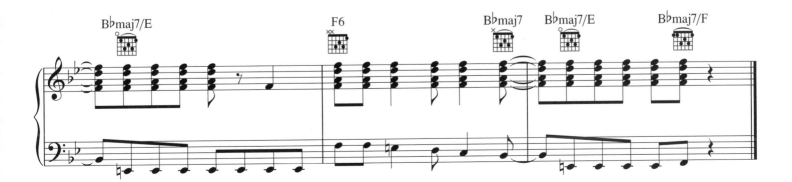

IT'S FIVE O'CLOCK SOMEWHERE

Words and Music by JIM BROWN
and DON ROLLINS

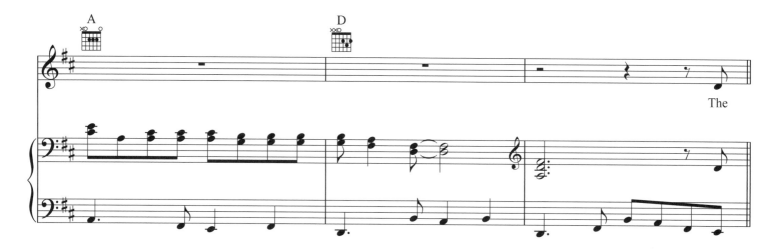

The

sun is hot ___ and that ___ old clock ___ is mov-in' slow and
this lunch break ___ is gon - na take ___ all af - ter - noon and

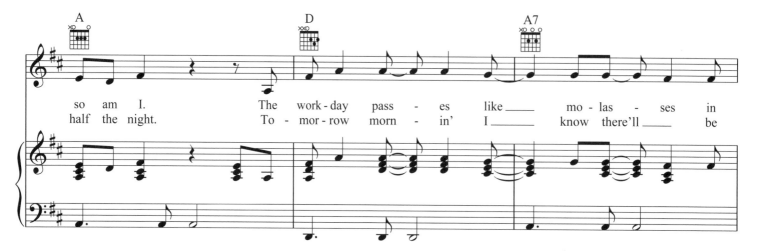

so am I. The work - day pass - es like ___ mo - las - ses in
half the night. To - mor - row morn - in' I ___ know there'll ___ be

win - ter time,　but it's Ju - ly.　I'm get - tin' paid　by the hou - r　and
hell to pay,　hey, but　that's al - right.　Ain't _ had　a day off now　in

old - er by　the min - ute.　My boss just　pushed _ me　o - ver the　lim - it. I'd like to
o - ver a　year.　My Ja - mai - can　va - ca - tion's gon - na　start right here.　If the

call him some - thin',　I think I'll　just call it a　day. ___ }
phone's for me,　you can　tell 'em　I've just sailed a - way. ___ }

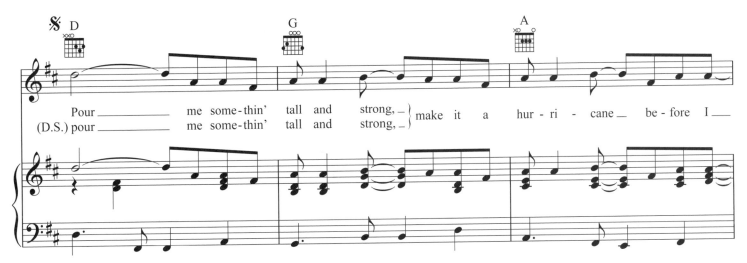

Pour ____　me some - thin' tall and　strong, _ } make it a hur - ri - cane _ be - fore I ____
(D.S.) pour ____　me some - thin' tall and　strong, _ }

_____ go in-sane. It's on-ly half_____ past twelve,_____ but I don't care._____

To Coda ⊕   N.C.

It's five_____ o'-clock some - where.

Well, it's five_____ o'-clock some - where.

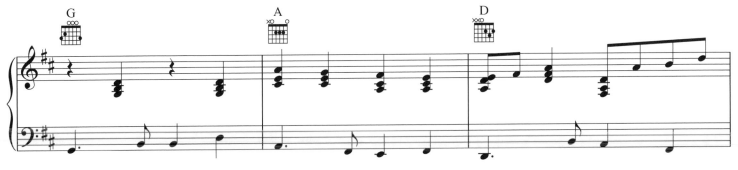

I could pay off my tab, pour my-self in a cab and be

back to work __ be-fore two. __ At a mo-ment like this, I

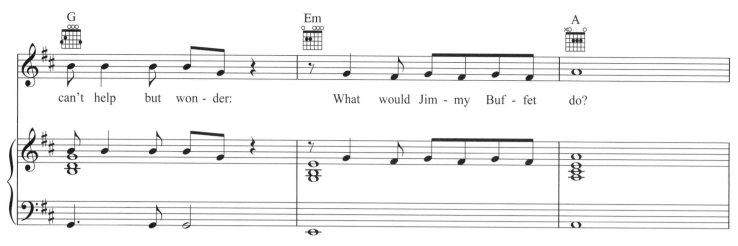

can't help but won - der: What would Jim - my Buf - fet do?

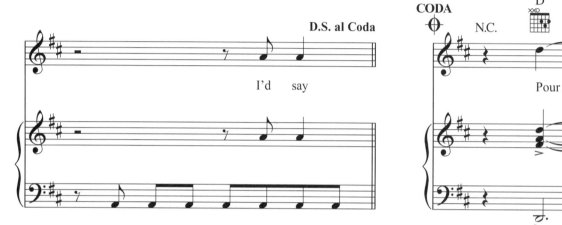

D.S. al Coda

I'd say

CODA

N.C.

Pour ___ me some - thin'

tall and strong, __ make it a hur - ri - cane __ be - fore I ___ go in - sane. It's

on - ly half ___ past twelve, __ but I don't care. ___

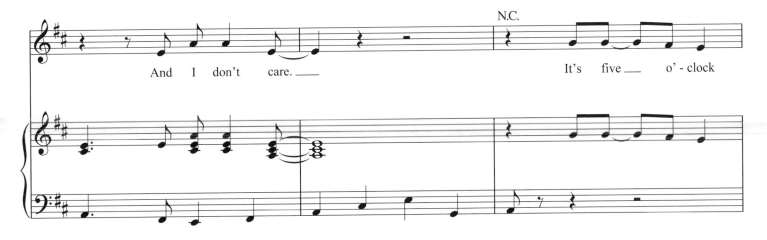

And I don't care. _____   It's five _____ o'-clock

some-where.

Repeat and Fade

ad lib.

Optional Ending

JAMMING

Words and Music by
BOB MARLEY

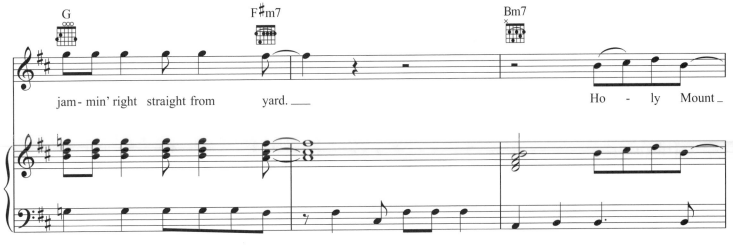

jam-min' right straight from yard. ___ Ho - ly Mount ___

___ Zi - on; Ho - ly Mount ___ Zi - on.

Jah sit - teth in Mount Zi - on and rules ___ all

cre - a - tion. Yeah, we're we're jam - min'. Bop - chu - wa - wa -

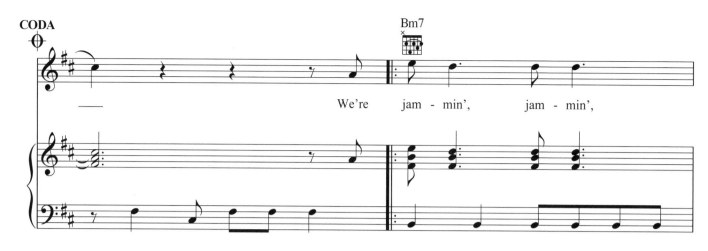

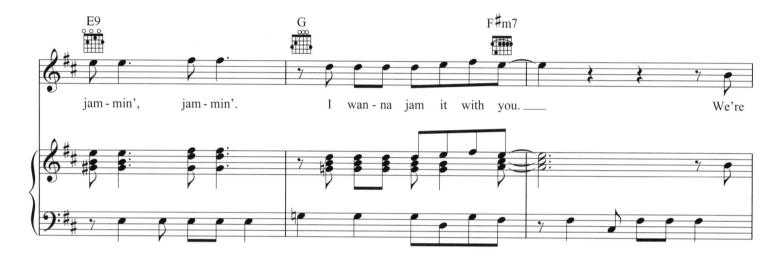

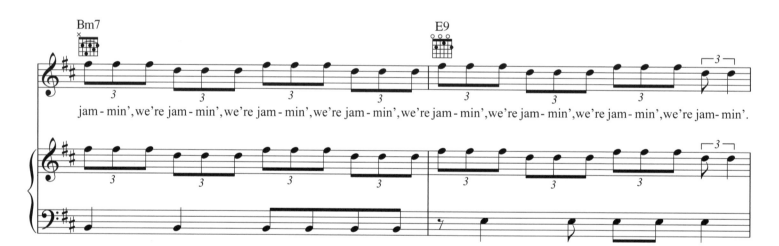

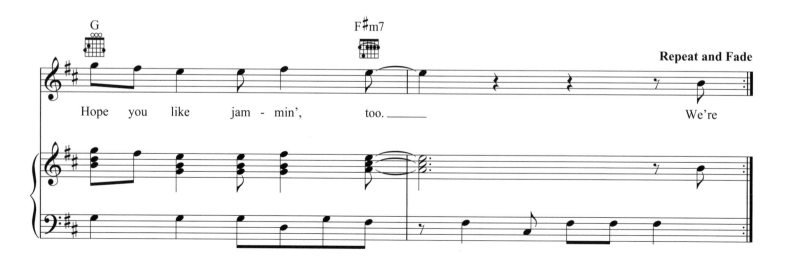

LOWDOWN

Words and Music by BOZ SCAGGS
and DAVID PAICH

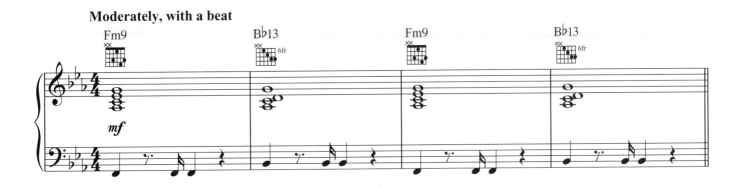

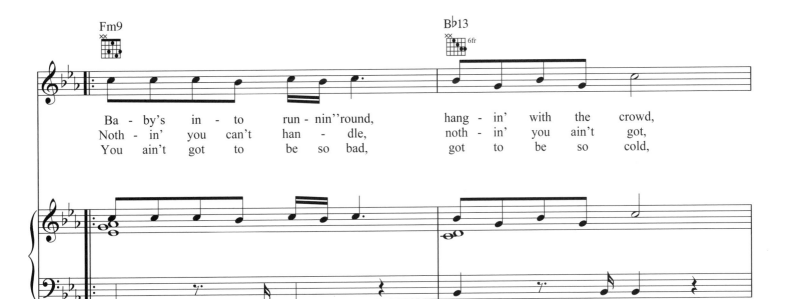

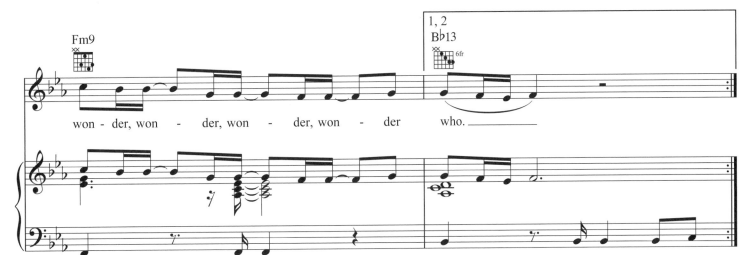

KOKOMO
from the Motion Picture COCKTAIL

Words and Music by JOHN PHILLIPS,
TERRY MELCHER, MIKE LOVE
and SCOTT McKENZIE

Moderately bright

A-ru-ba, Ja-mai-ca, oo ___ I wan-na take ya. Ber-mu-da, Ba-ha-ma, come ___

___ on, pret-ty ma-ma. Key Lar-go, Mon-te-go, ba-by, why don't we go, Ja-

mai-ca. Off the Flor-i-da Keys ___ We'll put out to sea ___

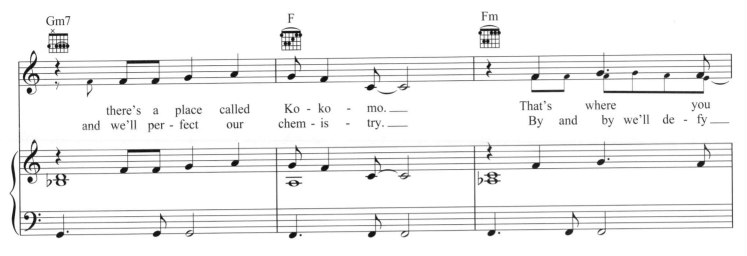

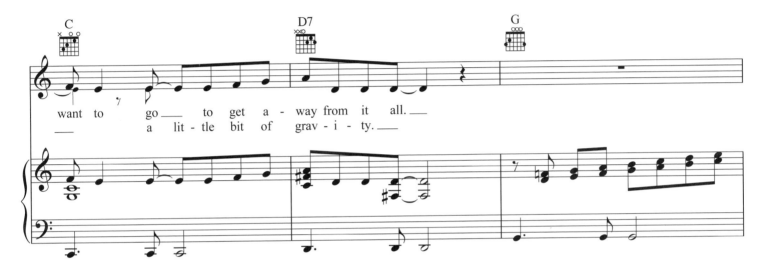

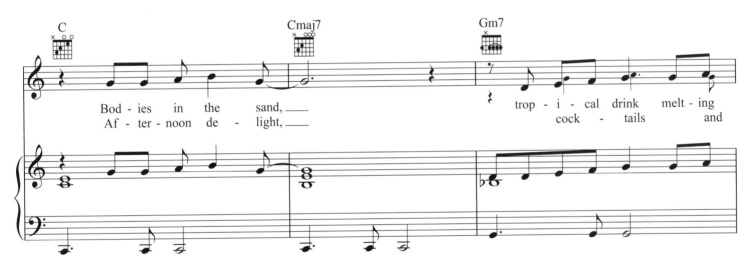

steel drum band ___ down in } Ko - ko - mo. ___
con - tact high ___ way down in } A - ru - ba Ja - mai - ca, oo ___

___ I wan - na take you to Ber - mu - da, Ba - ha - ma. Come ___

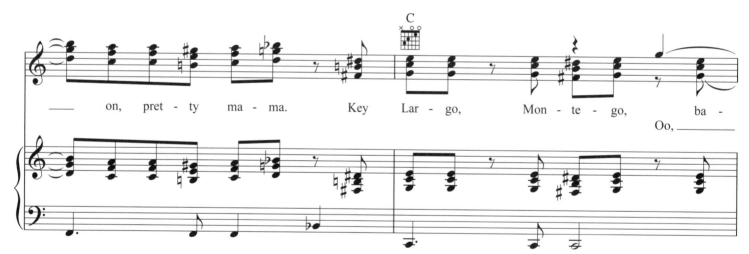

___ on, pret - ty ma - ma. Key Lar - go, Mon - te - go, ba - Oo, ___

- by, why don't we go?
___ I wan - na take you down to Ko - ko - mo. ___ We'll get there fast ___ and then we'll

take it slow. ___ That's where ___ we ___ wan - na go, _____

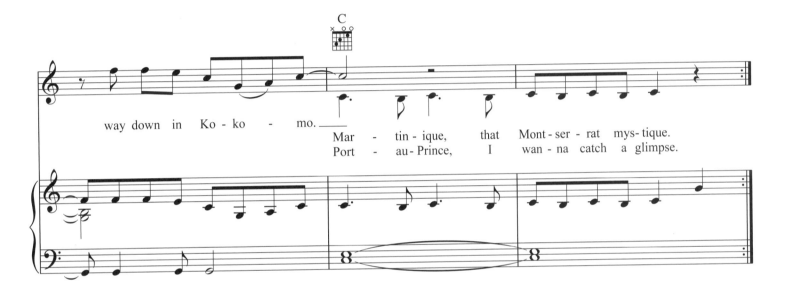

way down in Ko - ko - mo. ___

Mar - tin - ique,   that   Mont - ser - rat mys - tique.

Port - au - Prince,   I   wan - na catch a glimpse.

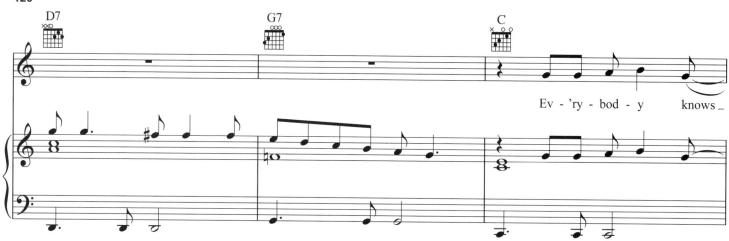

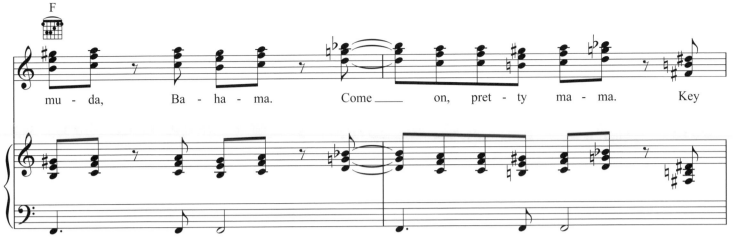

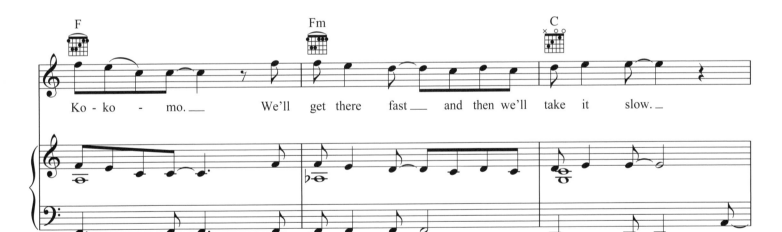

KU-U-I-PO
(Hawaiian Sweetheart)

Words and Music by LUIGI CREATORE,
GEORGE WEISS and HUGO PERETTI

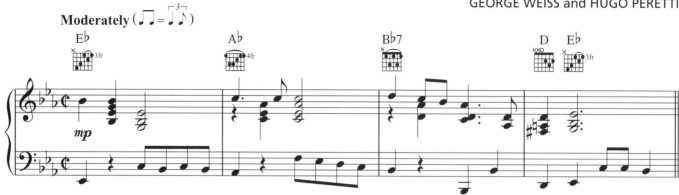

See the sweet Ha-wai-ian rose,   see it blos-som, see it
As the years go pass-ing by,   we'll re-call our wed-ding

grow.   That's the sto-ry of our love
day.   I will be there by your side.

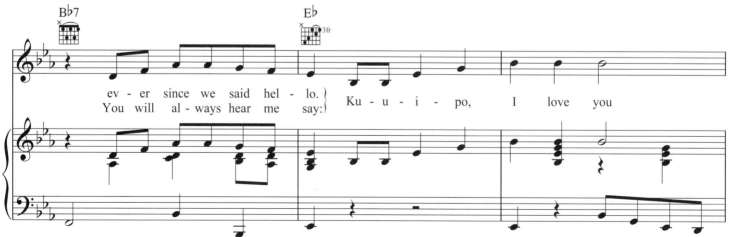

ev-er since we said hel-lo.   } Ku-u-i-po, I love you
You will al-ways hear me say: }

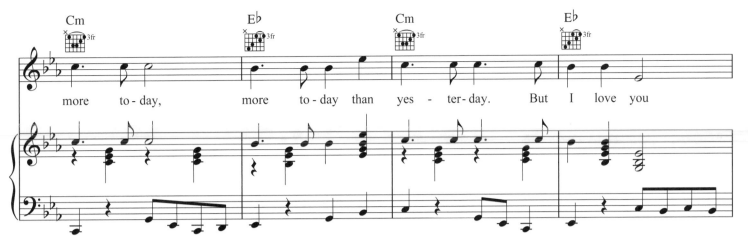

more to-day, more to-day than yes - ter-day. But I love you

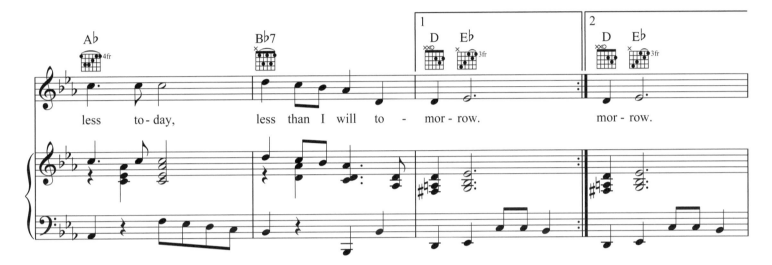

less to-day, less than I will to - mor - row. mor - row.

Ku - u - i - po, ku - u - i - po, you're my Ha - wai - ian sweet-heart.

Ku - u - i - po, ku - u - i - po, you're my Ha - wai - ian sweet-heart.

rall.

MAKIN' LOVE UKULELE STYLE

Words by CHARLIE HAYES
Music by PAUL WEIRICK

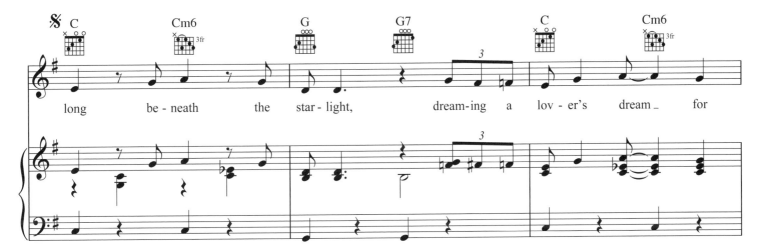

satisfy ___ the one you love ___ all else above, ___ take a

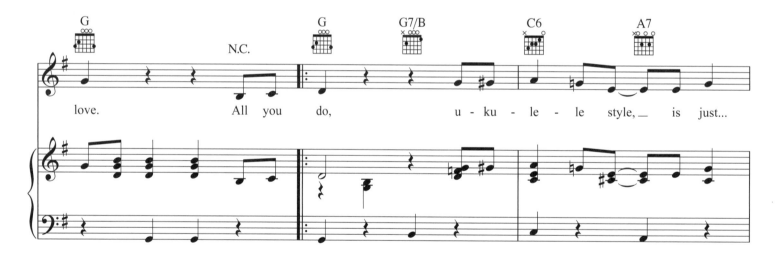

tip and be sure you try ___ the ukulele style of making

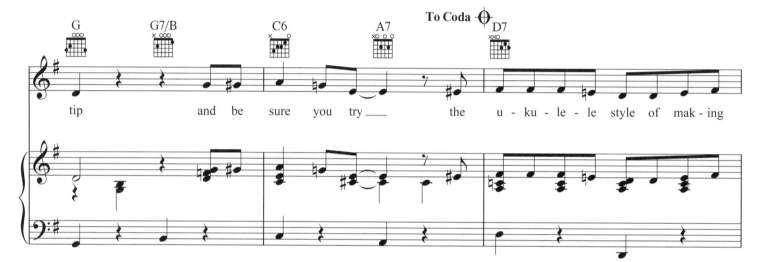

love. All you do, ukulele style, ___ is just...

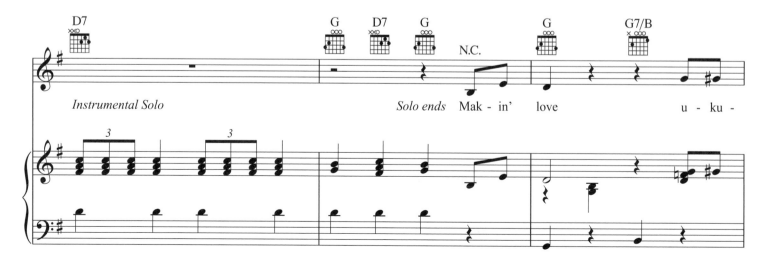

Instrumental Solo   *Solo ends* Makin' love uku-

THE MOON OF MANAKOORA
from the Motion Picture THE HURRICANE

Lyric by FRANK LOESSER
Music by ALFRED NEWMAN

The moon of Man-a-koo-ra filled _____ the night with

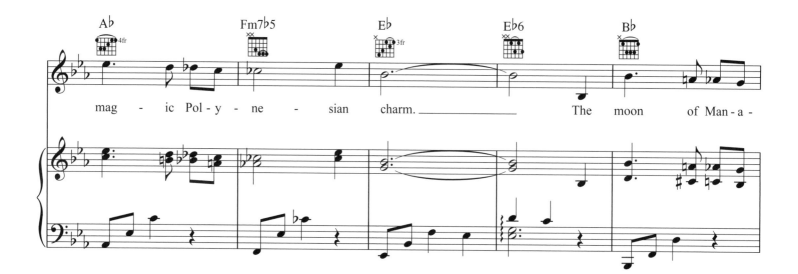

mag-ic Pol-y-ne-sian charm. _____ The moon of Man-a-

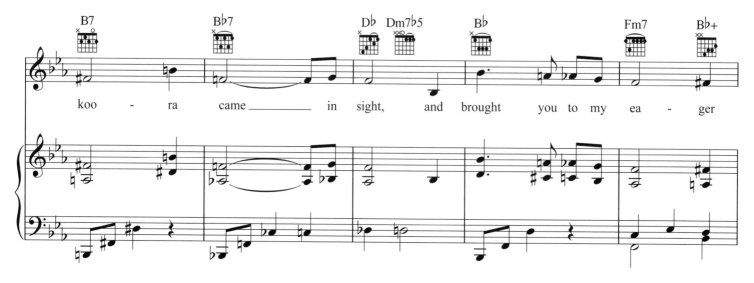

koo-ra came _____ in sight, and brought you to my ea-ger

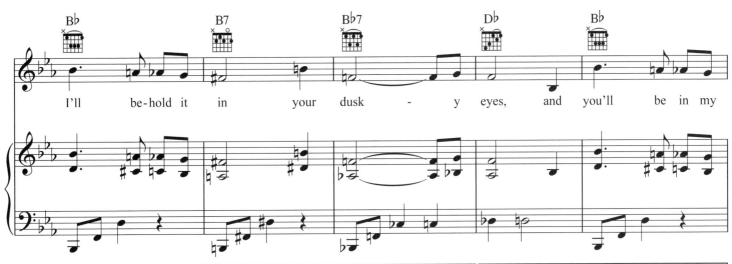

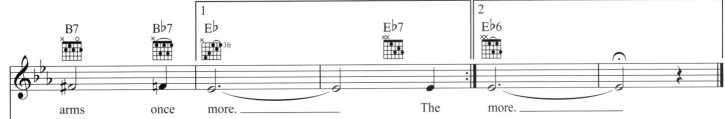

MY ISLAND HOME

Words and Music by
NEIL MURRAY

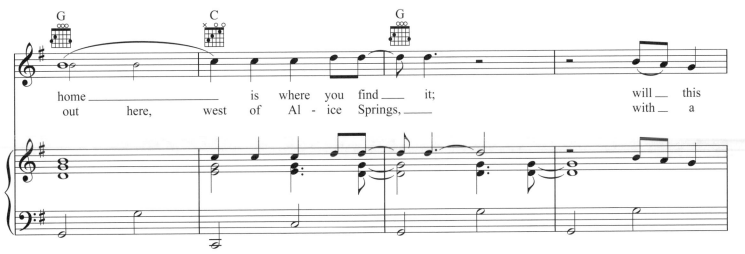

home _____ is where you find ___ it;
out here, _____ west of Al - ice Springs, ___

will ___ this
with ___ a

1, 3

place _____ ev - er sat - is - fy ____ me?
wife _____ and a fam - i - ly.

For I

2, 4

And my is - land home, ___

my is - land home, ___

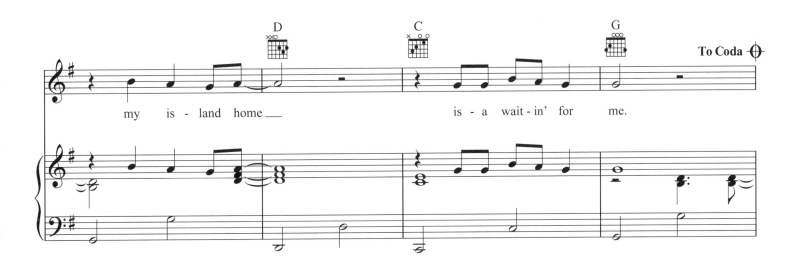

To Coda ⊕

my is - land home ___

is - a wait - in' for me.

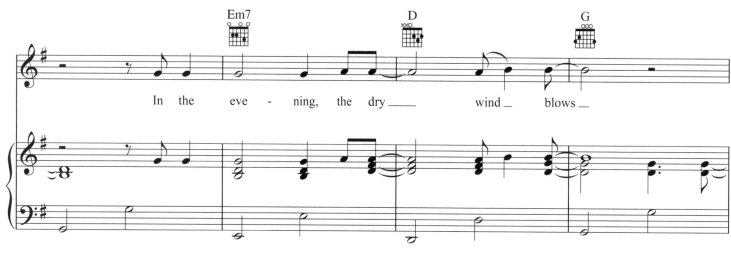

In the eve - ning, the dry ___ wind ___ blows ___

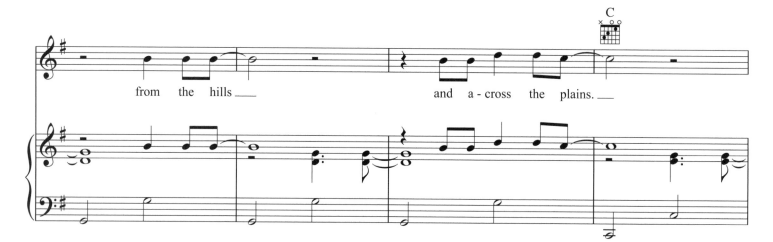

from the hills ___ and a - cross the plains. ___

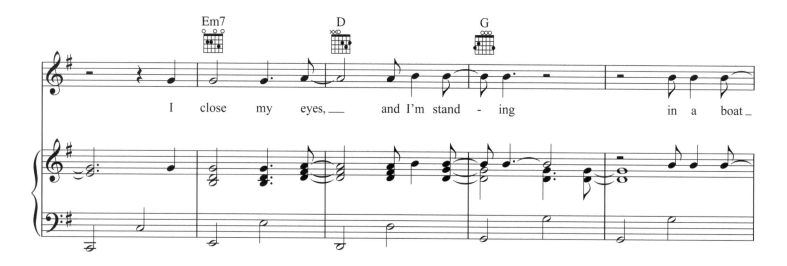

I close my eyes, ___ and I'm stand - ing in a boat ___

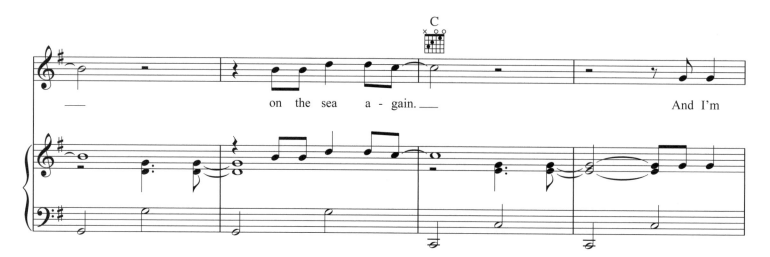

on the sea a - gain. ___ And I'm

hold - ing that long ___ tur - tle spear, ___ and I feel I'm close ___

___ now to where it must be. ___ My is - land home ___

is - a wait - in' for me.

D.S. al Coda (with repeat)

Straight-four feel

CODA

In the eve - ning, the dry ___ wind ___ blows ___

from the hills ___ and a-cross the plains. ___

I close my eyes, ___ and I'm stand - ing

in a boat ___ on the sea a - gain. ___ And I'm

hold - ing that long ___ tur - tle spear, ___ and I feel I'm close ___

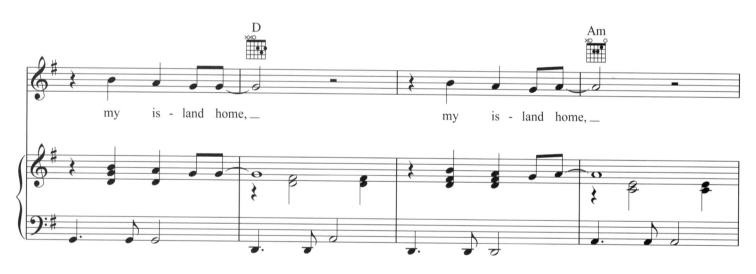

MY ISLAND PARADISE

Words and Music by WEBLEY EDWARDS,
W.H. MILLER and LEON POBER

Languidly, slowly

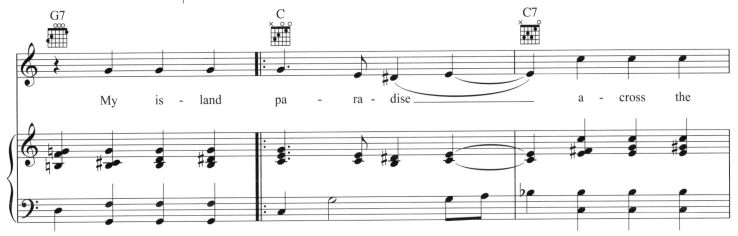

My is - land pa - ra - dise _____ a - cross the

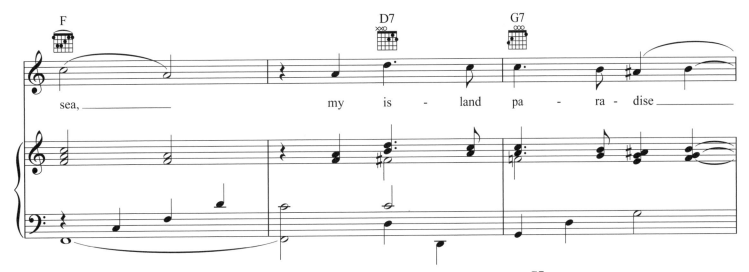

sea, _____ my is - land pa - ra - dise _____

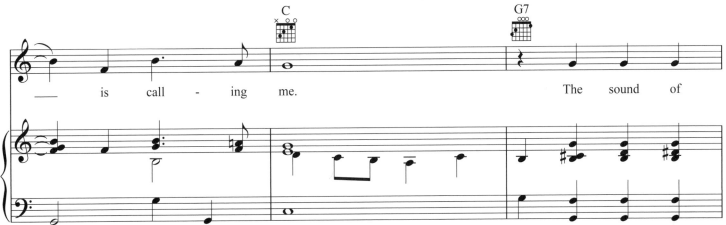

_____ is call - ing me. The sound of

soft gui - tars, _____ the scent of spice _____

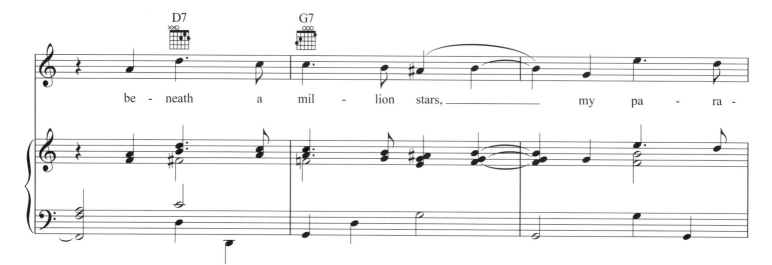

be - neath a mil - lion stars, _____ my pa - ra -

dise. _____ The waves up - on the shore _____ whis - per their

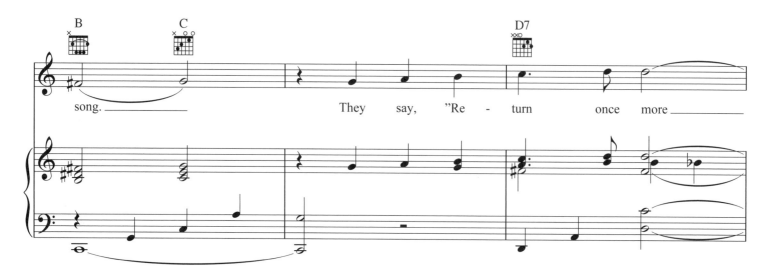

song. _____ They say, "Re - turn once more _____

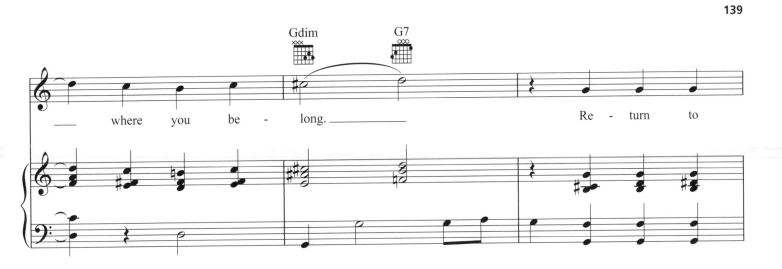

where you be - long. _____ Return to

pa - ra - dise _____ a - cross the sea." _____

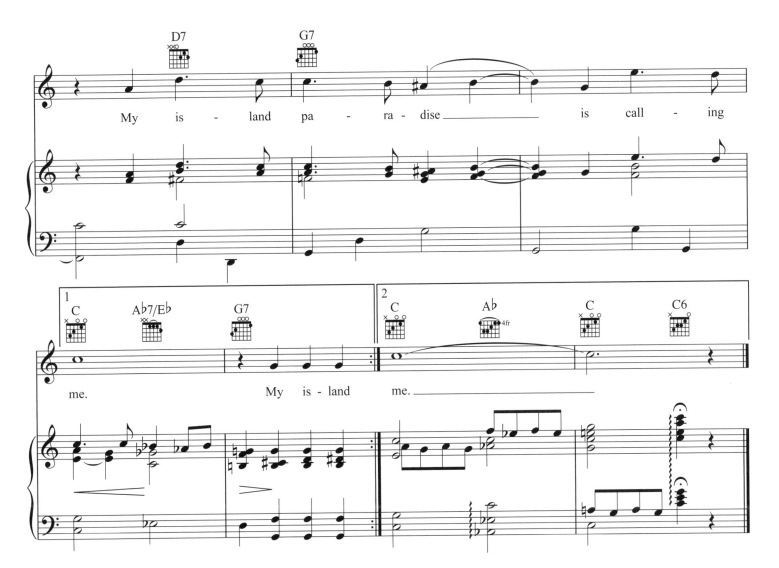

My is - land pa - ra - dise _____ is call - ing

me. My is - land me. _____

NO SHOES NO SHIRT
(No Problems)

Words and Music by
CASEY BEATHARD

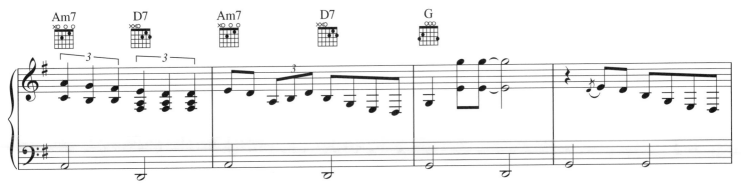

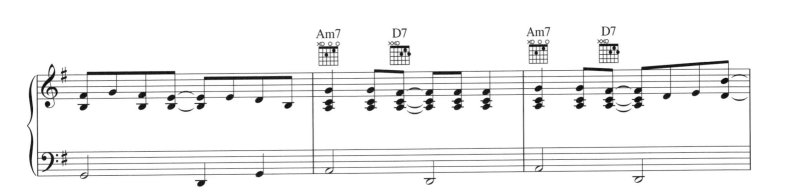

I've been up _____ to my neck ___ work-in' six ___
_____ on a chair ___ and the sand ___

_____ days a week, _____ wear-in' holes in the soles _____ of the shoes _____ on my feet. _____ Been
_____ by the sea. _____ Wan-na look through my shades _____ and see you _____ there with me. _____ Wan-na

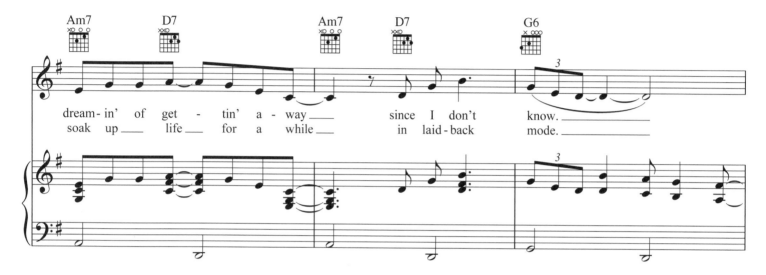

dream-in' of get-tin' a-way _____ since I don't know. _____
soak up _____ life _____ for a while _____ in laid-back mode. _____

Ain't no _____ bet-ter time _____ than now _____ for Mex-i-co. _____
No _____ boss, _____ no clock, _____ no _____ stress, no dress code. _____

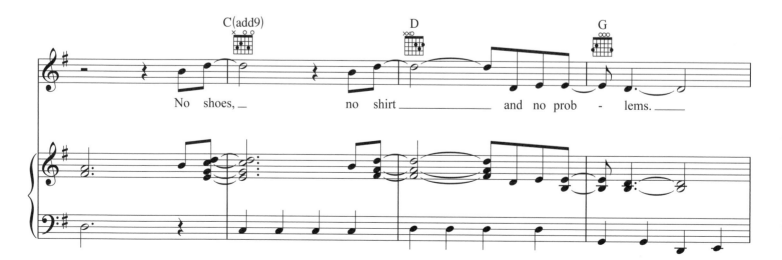

No shoes, _____ no shirt _____ and no prob - lems. _____

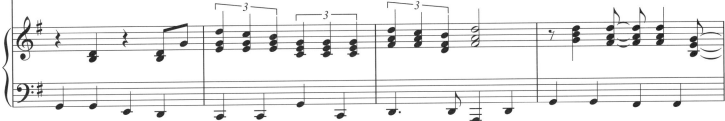

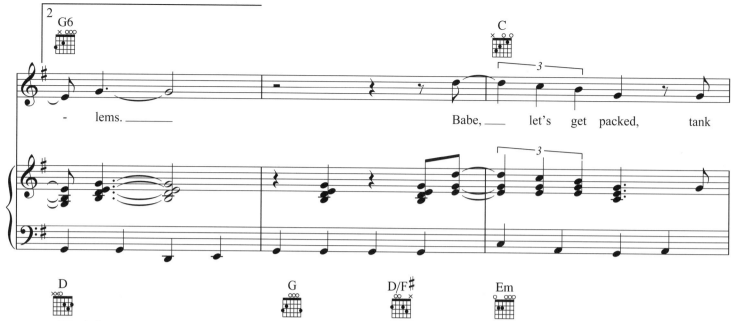

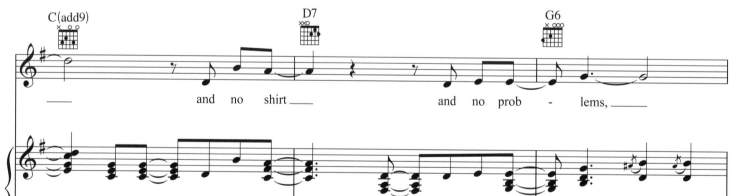

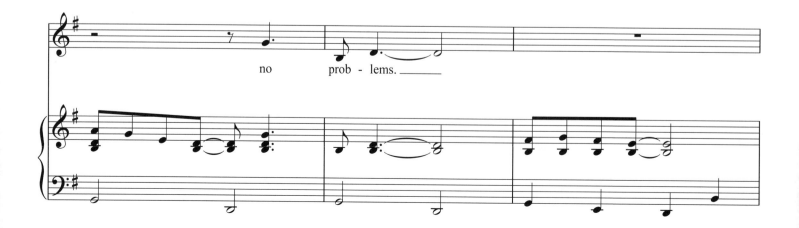

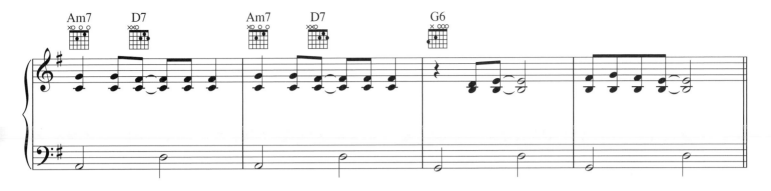

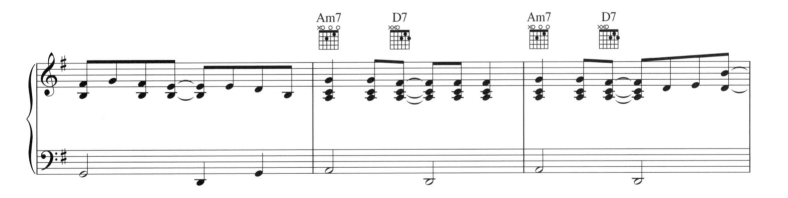

NO WOMAN NO CRY

Words and Music by
VINCENT FORD

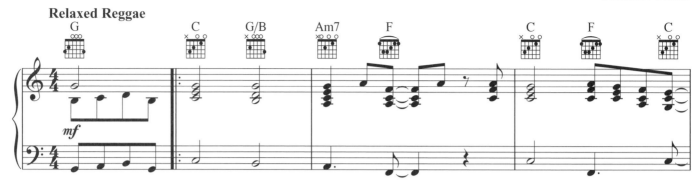

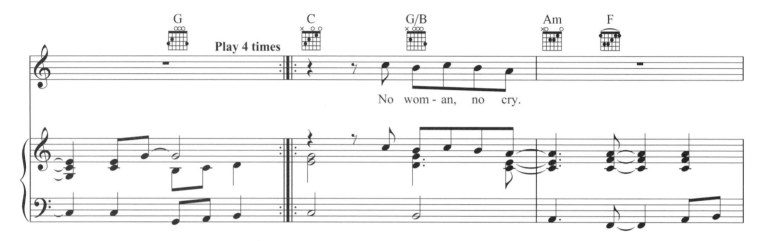

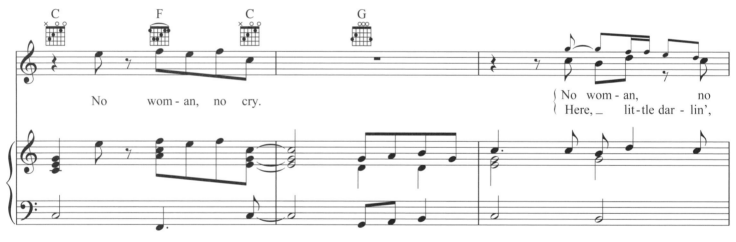

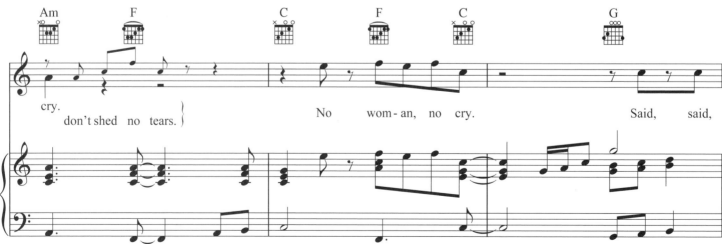

said I re-mem-ber)
(D.S.) Said I re-mem-ber)
when we used __ to sit

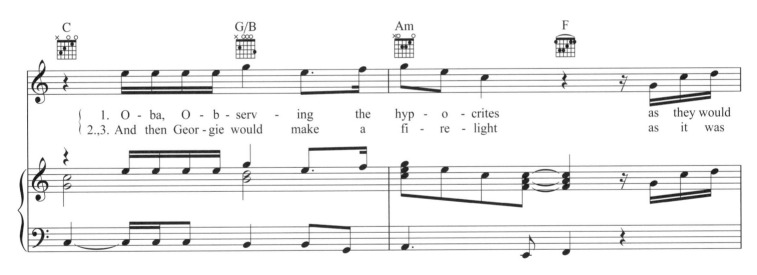

in the gov-ern-ment yard in Trench-town.

1. O-ba, O-b-serv - ing the hyp-o-crites   as they would
2.,3. And then Geor-gie would make a fi-re-light   as it was

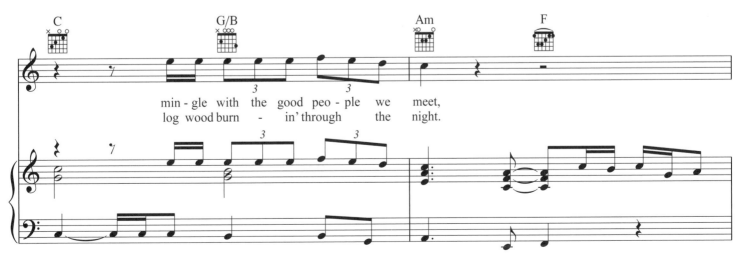

min-gle with the good peo-ple we meet,
log wood burn - in' through the night.

good friends __ we had, _____ oh, good friends we've lost _____
Then we ____ would cook ____ corn - meal por - ridge

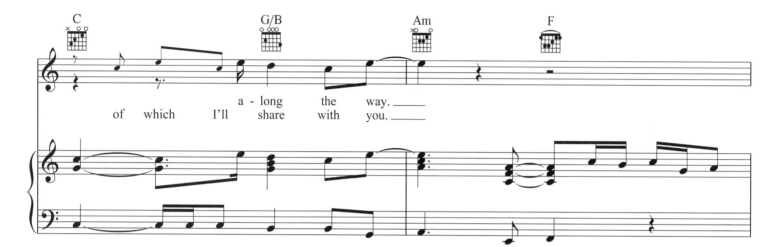

_____ a - long the way. _____
of which I'll share with you. _____

In ___ this bright __ fu - ture you ___ can't for - get your __ past,
My feet __ is my on - ly ___ car - riage, _____

To Coda ⊕

so, dry your tears ___ I _____ say. And
so, I've got to push on _____ through. But while I'm gone, I mean...

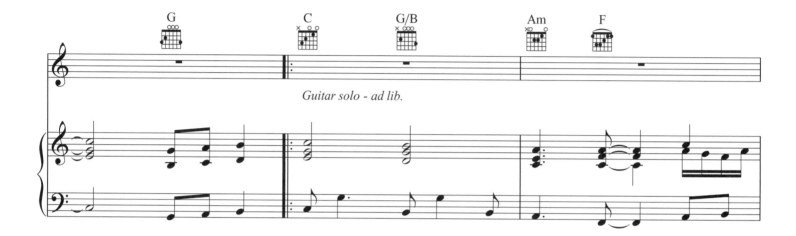

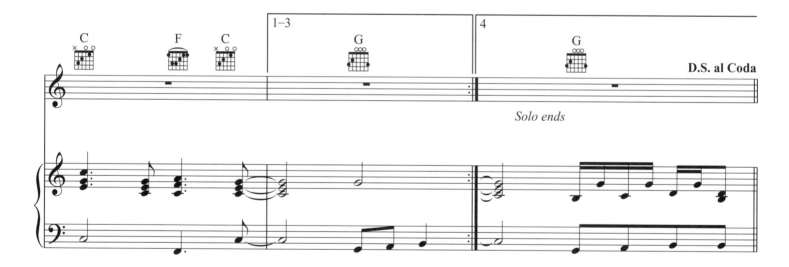

Oh, my lit-tle dar-lin', I say don't shed no tears.

No wom-an, no cry.

Yeah.

Lit-tle dar-lin',
Vocal tacet 3rd time

Play 3 times

don't shed no tears. _____

No wom-an, no cry.

ONE LOVE

Words and Music by
BOB MARLEY

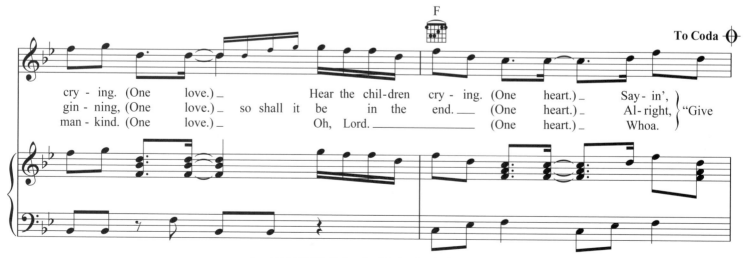

thanks and praise to the Lord and I will feel all right." Say - in',

"Let's get to - geth - er and feel all right." Whoa, whoa, whoa, whoa.
One more thing.

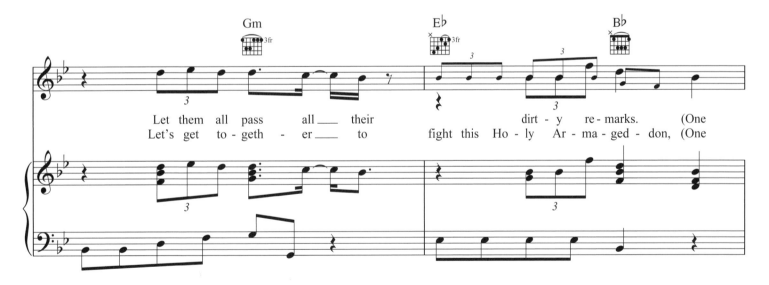

Let them all pass all ___ their dirt - y re - marks. (One
Let's get to - geth - er ___ to fight this Ho - ly Ar - ma - ged - don, (One

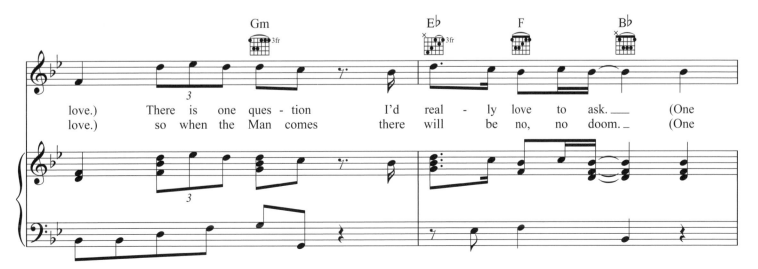

love.) There is one ques - tion I'd real - ly love to ask. ___ (One
love.) so when the Man comes there will be no, no doom. __ (One

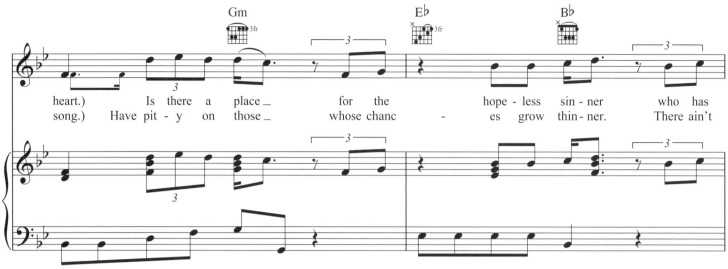

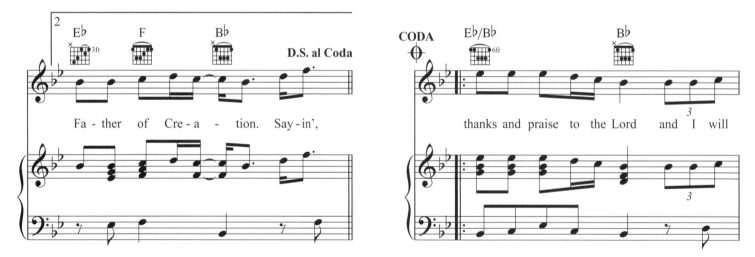

ONE PADDLE, TWO PADDLE

Words and Music by
KUI LEE

CODA

Sing-ing: One pad-dle, two pad-dle, three pad-dle for to take me home. __ Sing-ing: One pad-dle, two pad-dle, three pad-dle for to take me home. _____

ONE MORE ALOHA

Words and Music by
EDDIE LUND

One more a - lo - ha, _____ my love - ly is - land flow'r.
lo - ha, _____ be - fore the part - ing hour;

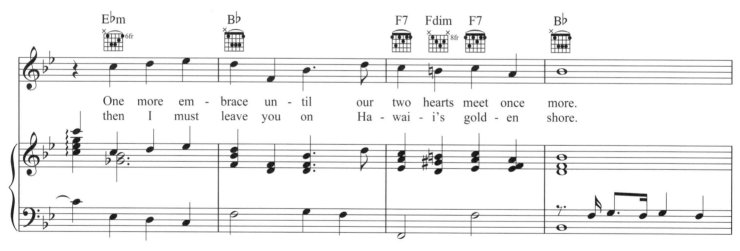

One more em - brace un - til our two hearts meet once more.
then I must leave you on Ha - wai - i's gold - en shore.

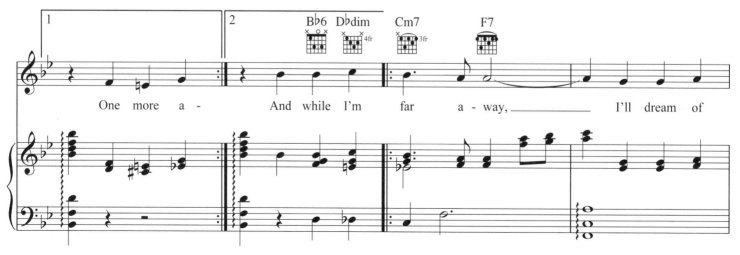

1.
One more a -

2.
And while I'm far a - way, _____ I'll dream of

you each day. You'll find my heart is there _____ in your ten - der

care. _____ One part - ing kiss, dear, _____ from lips that

I a - dore. One more a - lo - ha till you're in my arms once

more. And while I'm more. _____

OVER THE RAINBOW
from THE WIZARD OF OZ

Music by HAROLD ARLEN
Lyric by E.Y. "YIP" HARBURG

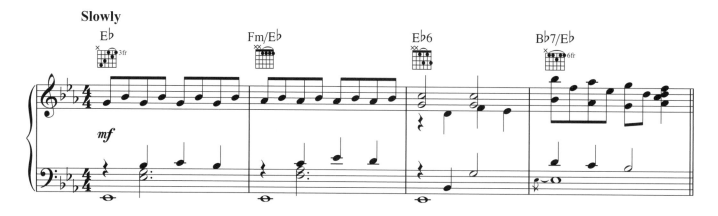

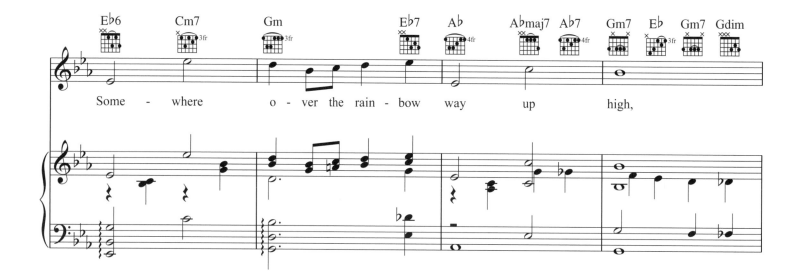

Some - where o - ver the rain - bow way up high,

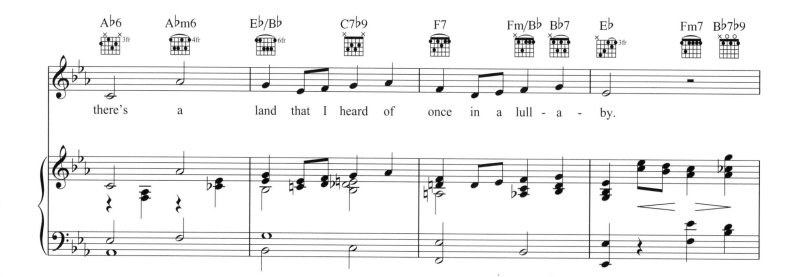

there's a land that I heard of once in a lull - a - by.

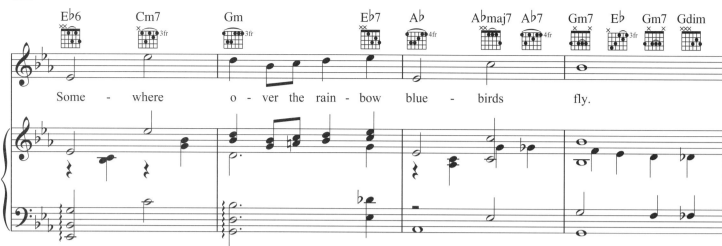

Some - where o - ver the rain - bow blue - birds fly.

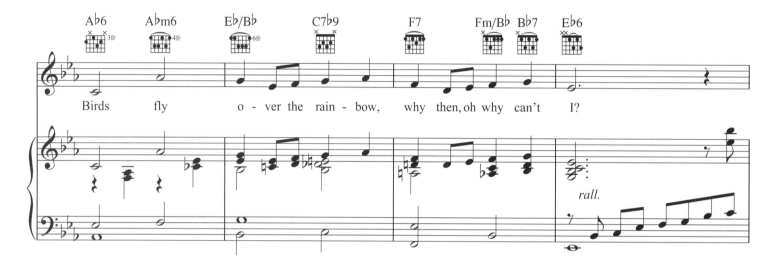

Birds fly o - ver the rain - bow, why then, oh why can't I?

rall.

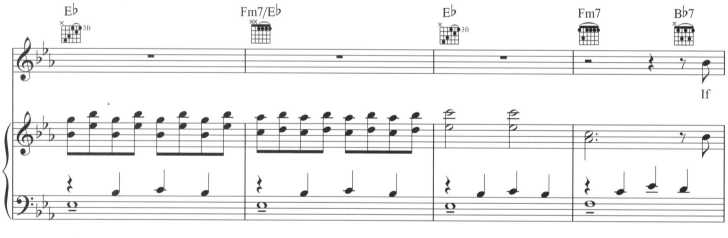

If

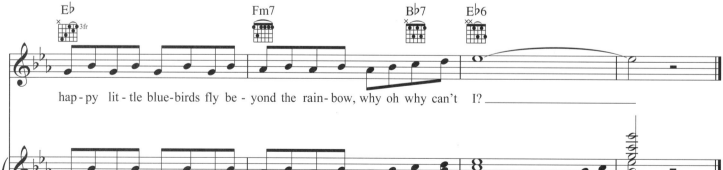

hap - py lit - tle blue-birds fly be - yond the rain - bow, why oh why can't I? _____

rit. **pp** *L.H.*

QUIET VILLAGE

By LES BAXTER

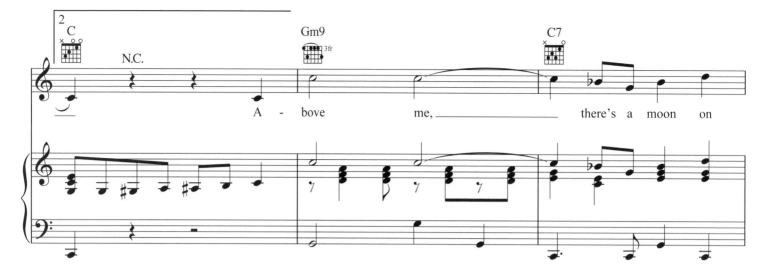

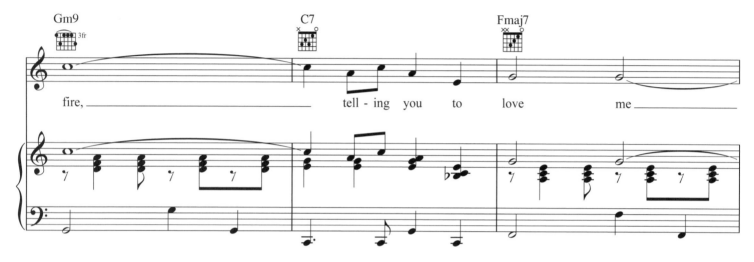

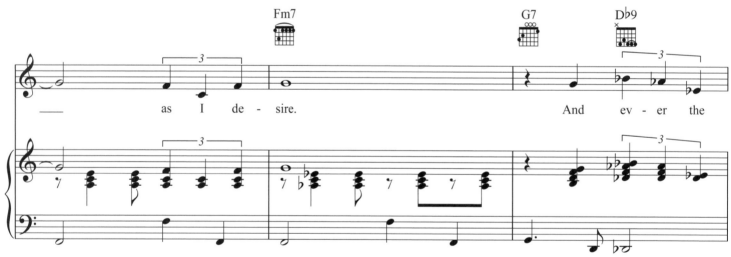

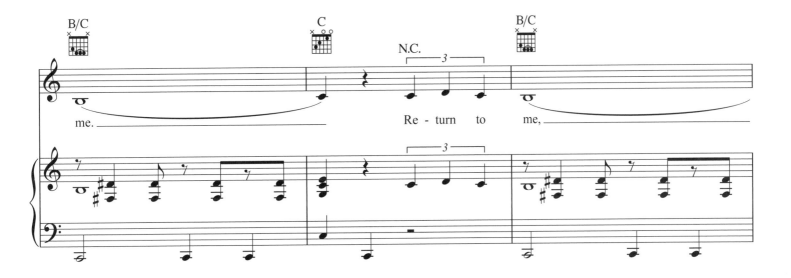

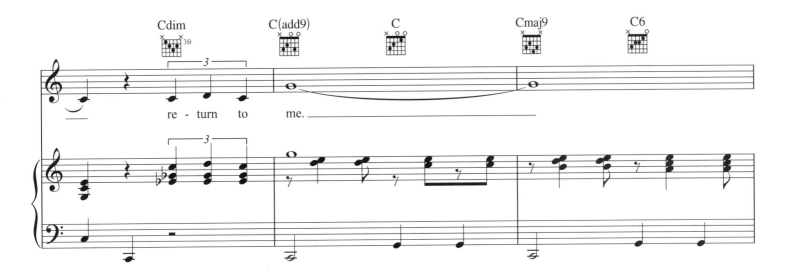

PEARLY SHELLS
(Pupu O Ewa)

Words and Music by WEBLEY EDWARDS
and LEON POBER

Pearl-y shells _____ from the o-cean _____ shin-ing in the

sun, _____ cov-er-ing the shore. _____ When I see them, _____

—— my heart tells me that I love you more than all the

lit - tle pearl - y shells. For ev - 'ry grain of sand up-

on the beach, I've got a kiss for you; and I've got more left o - ver for each star that

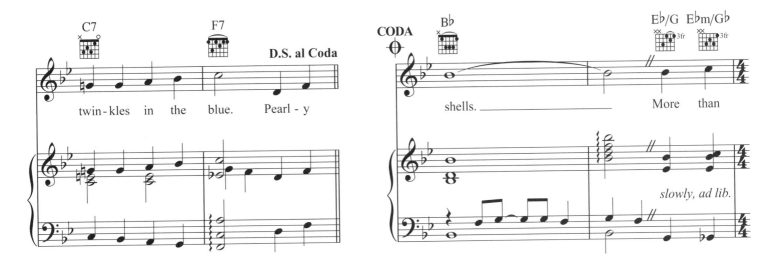

twin-kles in the blue. Pearl - y

shells. More than

all the lit - tle pearl - y shells.

RED, RED WINE

Words and Music by
NEIL DIAMOND

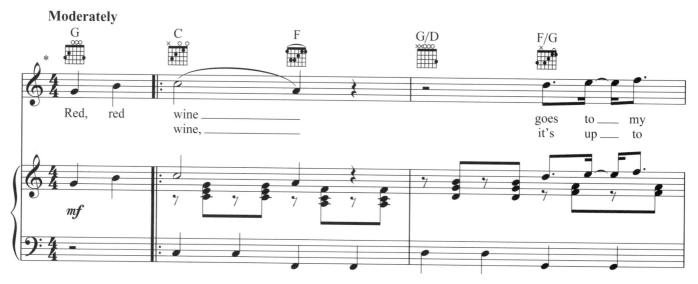

* Recorded a half step higher

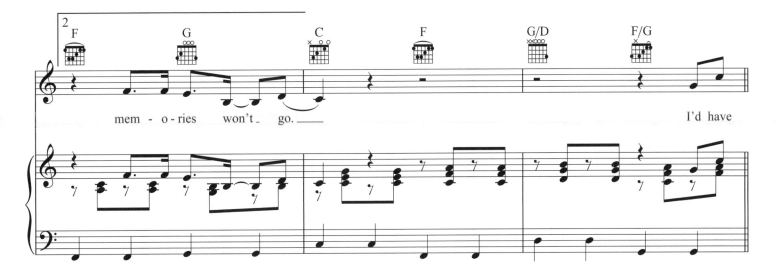

mem - o - ries won't _ go. ____ I'd have

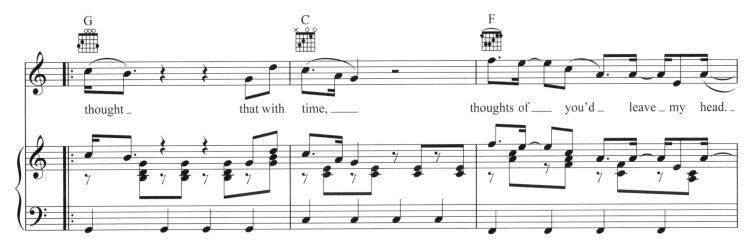

thought _ that with time, ____ thoughts of ___ you'd _ leave _ my head. _

____ I was wrong; ____ now I ____ find ____ just one

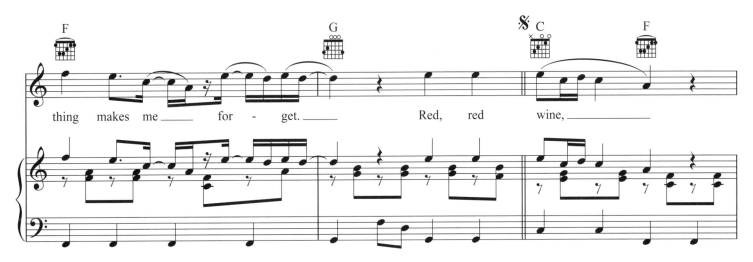

thing makes me ____ for - get. ___ Red, red wine, ____

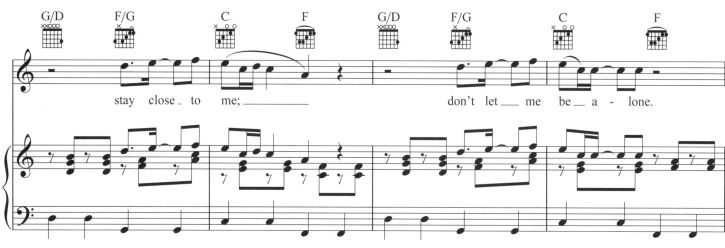

stay close _ to me; ___ don't let _ me be _ a - lone.

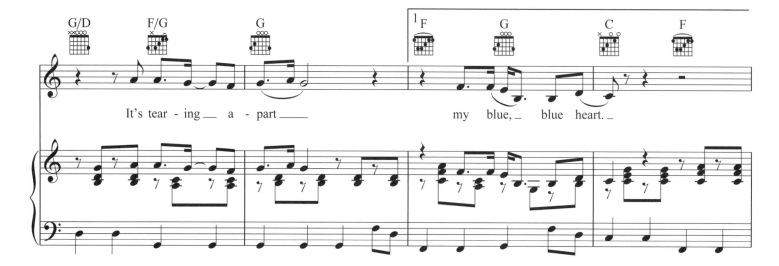

It's tear - ing _ a - part ___ my blue, _ blue heart. _

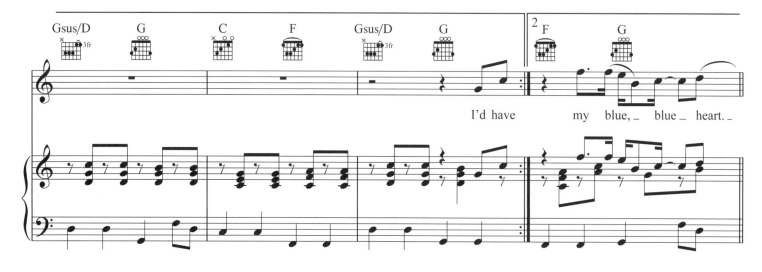

I'd have my blue, _ blue _ heart. _

D.S. and Fade

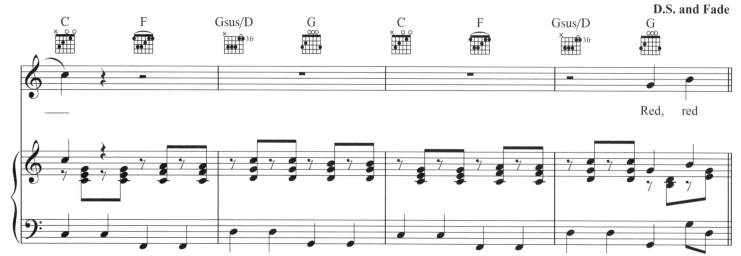

Red, red

REDEMPTION SONG

Words and Music by
BOB MARLEY

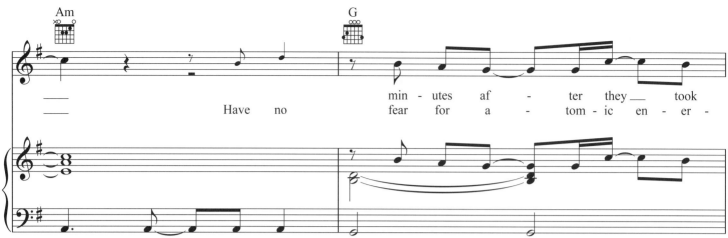

Am / G

min - utes af - ter they ___ took
Have no   fear for a - tom - ic en - er -

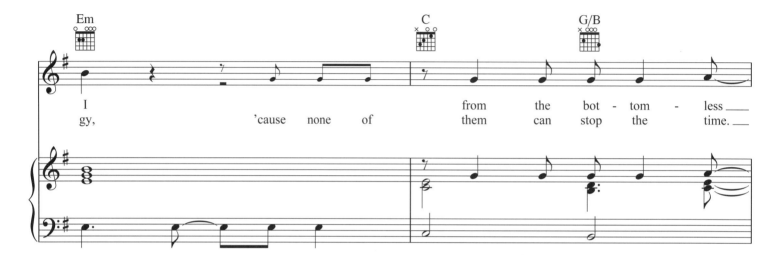

Em / C / G/B

I   from the bot - tom - less ___
gy,   'cause none of   them can stop the   time. ___

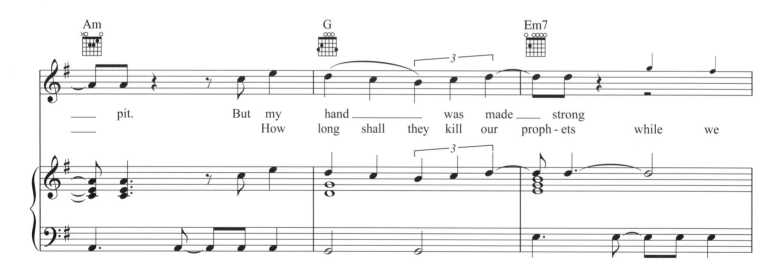

Am / G / Em7

___ pit.   But my hand ___ was made ___ strong
How long shall they kill our proph - ets   while we

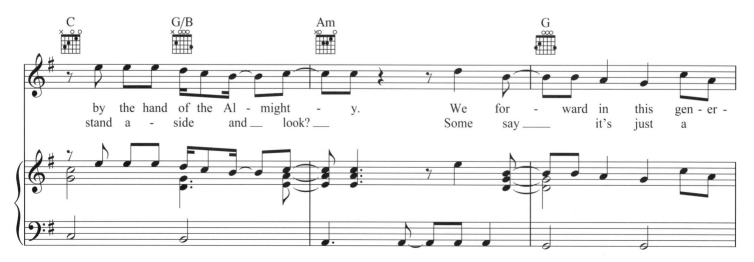

C / G/B / Am / G

by the hand of the Al - might - y.   We for - ward in this gen - er -
stand a - side and ___ look? ___ Some say ___ it's just a

a - tion ____ tri - umph - ant - ly.
part of it. We've got to ful - fill the ___ book.

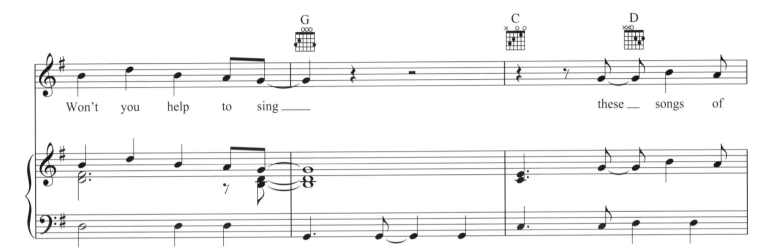

Won't you help to sing ___ these __ songs of

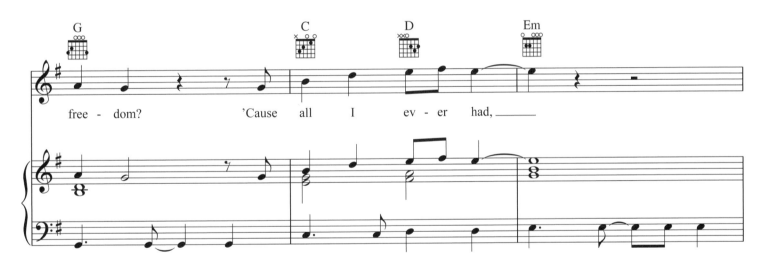

free - dom? 'Cause all I ev - er had, _____

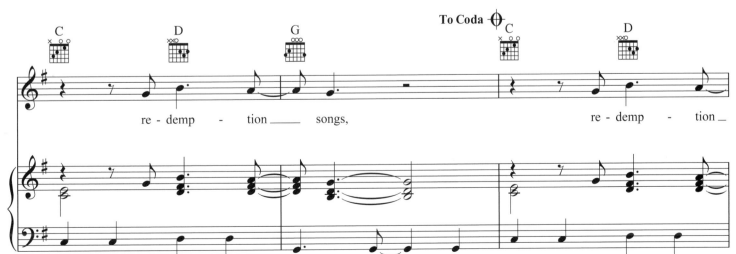

re - demp - tion ___ songs, re - demp - tion ___

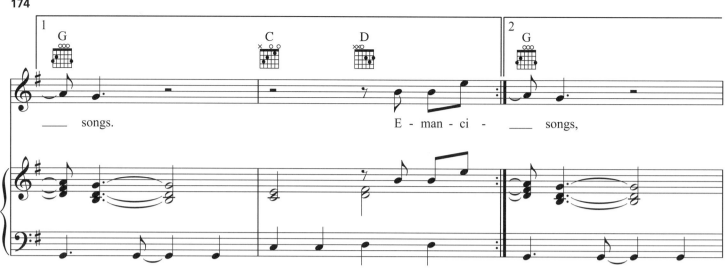

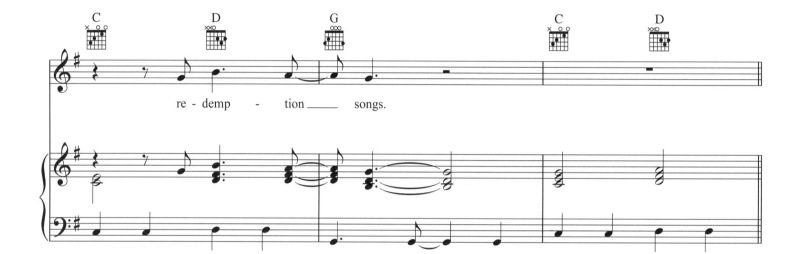

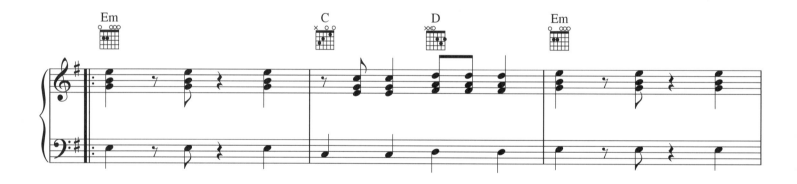

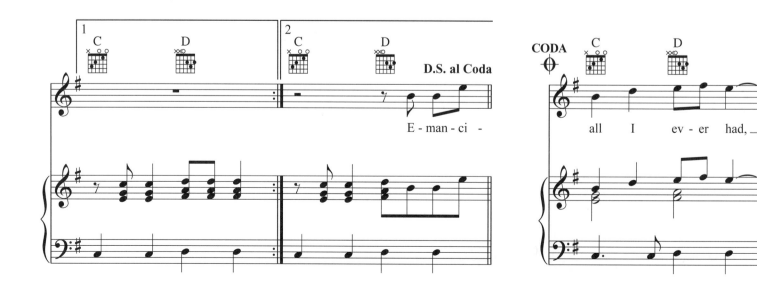

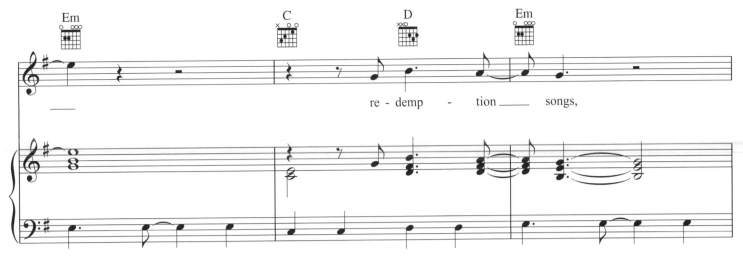

re - demp - tion _____ songs,

these __ songs of free - dom, songs of free -

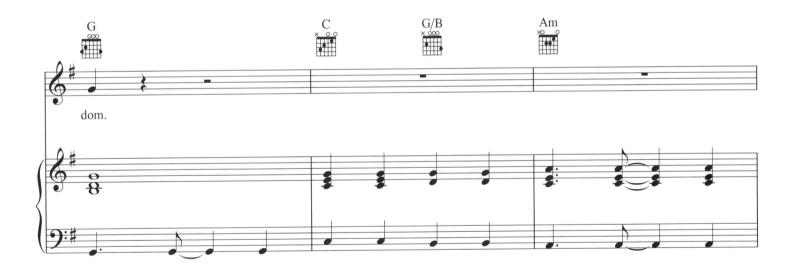

dom.

RED SAILS IN THE SUNSET

Words by JIMMY KENNEDY
Music by HUGH WILLIAMS (WILL GROSZ)

'Twas down, where fish-er folk gath-er, I
Red sails, where the night breeze is blow-ing, and

wan - dered far from the throng. I heard a fish-er girl
clouds are hid-ing the moon. A-bove no bright stars are

sing - ing and this re-frain was her song:
glow - ing; it means the storm's com-ing soon:

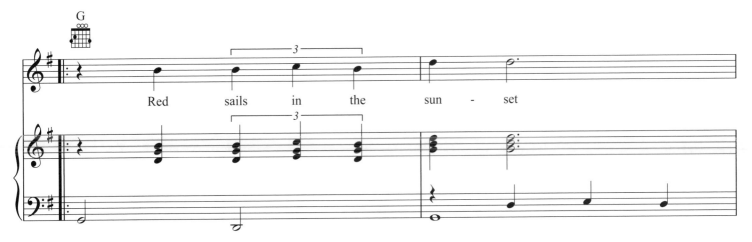

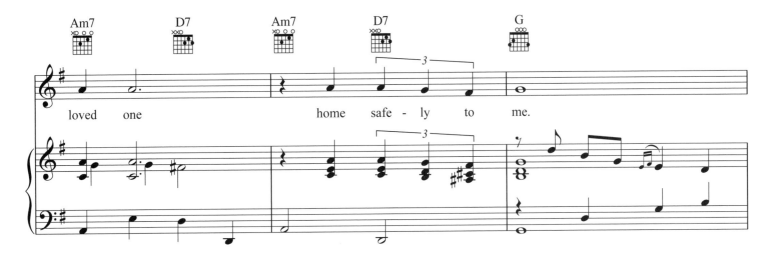

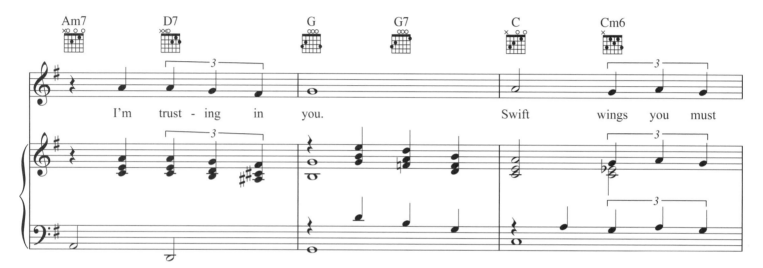

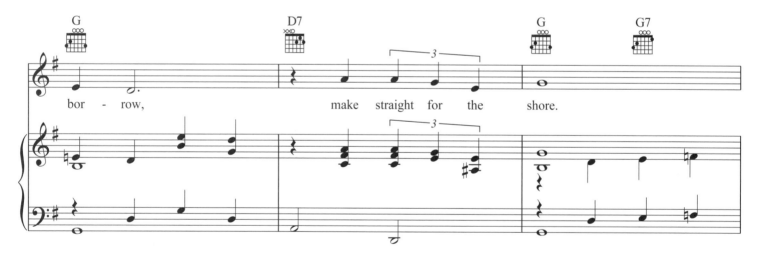

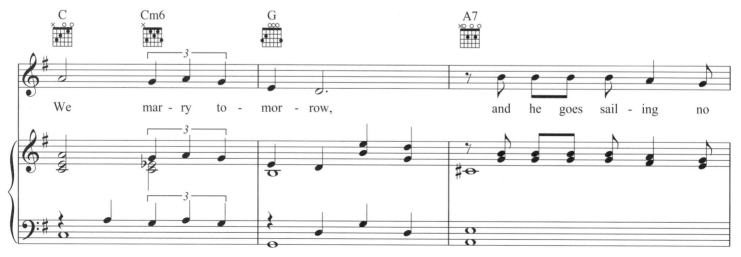

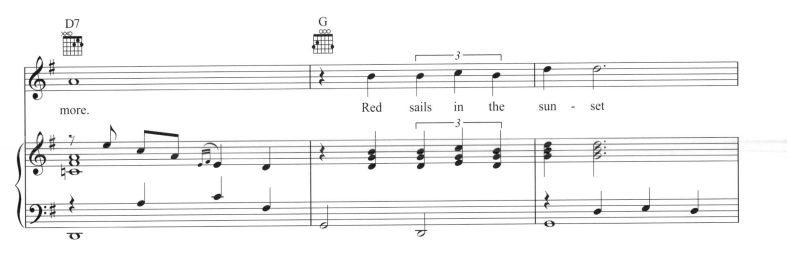

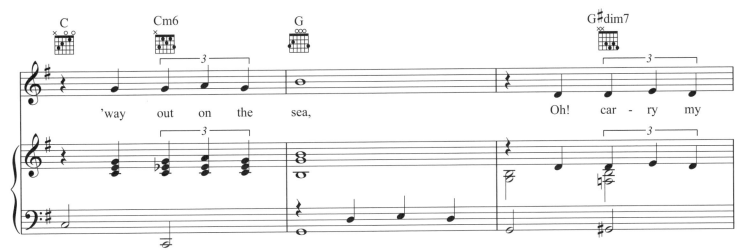

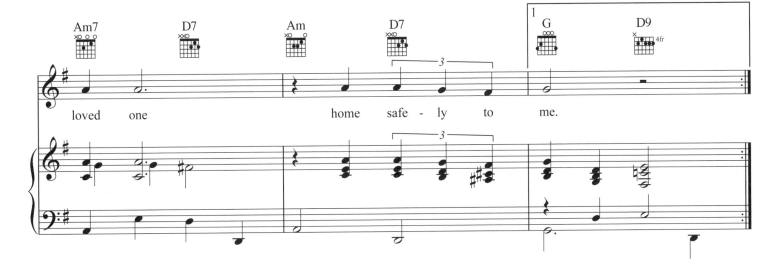

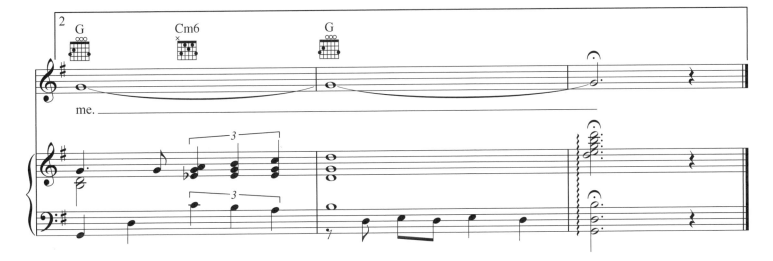

RIVERS OF BABYLON

Words and Music by BRENT DOWE,
JAMES A. McNAUGHTON, GEORGE REYAM
and FRANK FARIAN

By the riv-ers of Bab-y-lon___ where He sat down

and there He wept___ when He re-mem-bers

Zi - on. _____ 'Cause the wick - ed _____ car - ried us a - way, cap -

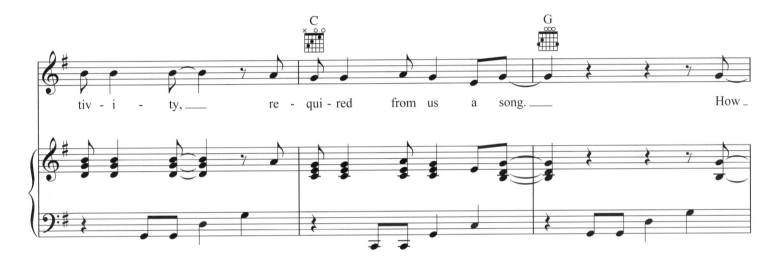

tiv - i - ty, _____ re - qui - red from us a song. _____ How _____

_____ can we sing King of _____ our song _____ in a strange _____ land? _

_____ 'Cause the wick - ed _____ car - ried us a - way, cap -

tiv-i-ty, ___ re-qui-red from us a song. ___ How _

___ can we sing King of ___ our song _ in a strange _____ land? _

(Ah.) ___ Sing it out loud. ___ (Ah.) ___ Sing a song of free-dom, {broth - er. / sis - ter.}

(Ah.) _____ Sing a song of free-dom, {bro - broth - er. ___ / sis - sis - ter. ___}

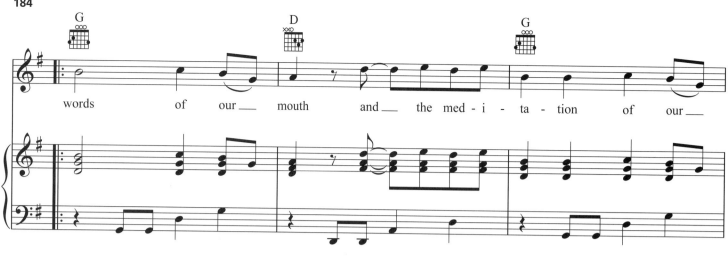

words of our ___ mouth and ___ the med - i - ta - tion of our ___

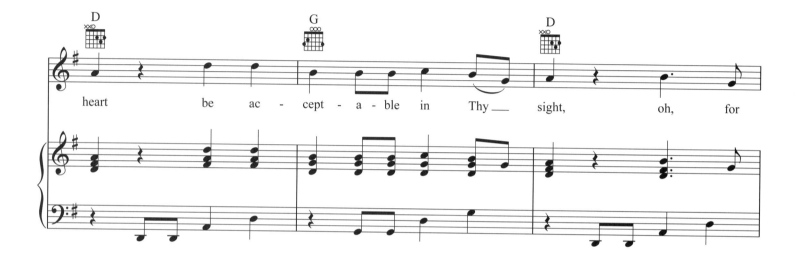

heart be ac - cept - a - ble in Thy ___ sight, oh, for

right. ___ (Ah.) So let the right. ___ Sing it out loud. ___

(Ah.) ___ We got to sing ___ it to - geth - er. (Ah.) ___

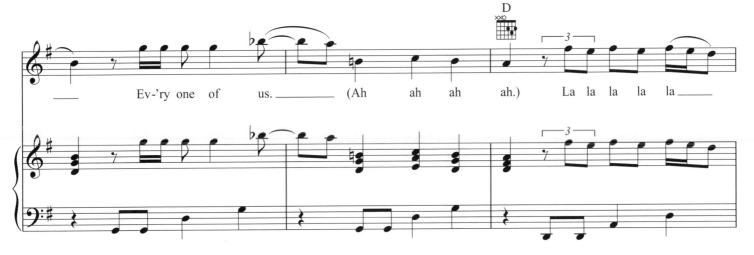

Ev-'ry one of us. ____ (Ah ah ah ah.) La la la la la ____

la la. (Ah ah ah ah.) Whoa __ whoa ____ whoa. ___ (Ah.) ____

____ (Ah.) ____

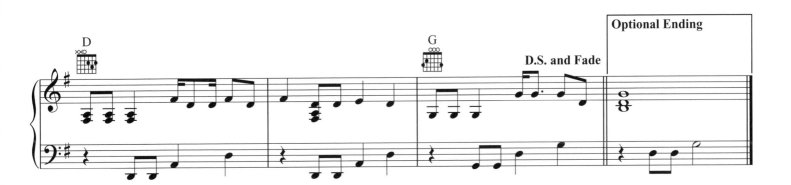

Optional Ending

D.S. and Fade

SEA BREEZE

By AL HOFFMAN,
DICK MANNING and IRMGARD ALULI

Moderately, with feeling

Sea breeze, sea breeze, take a mes-sage to the one I love. __ Kiss her ten-der-ly, tell her to wait for me, and say that I'll be com-ing soon __

to meet her by the blue la - goon. Sea breeze,

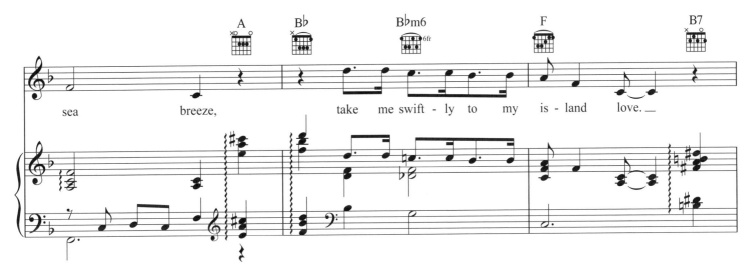

sea breeze, take me swift - ly to my is - land love. __

Make the breez - es strong; I've been a - way too long from lips and arms that I a -

dore, _____ from all that I've been long - ing for.

Soothe her, if you should find her cry - ing.

Whis - per my love for her has

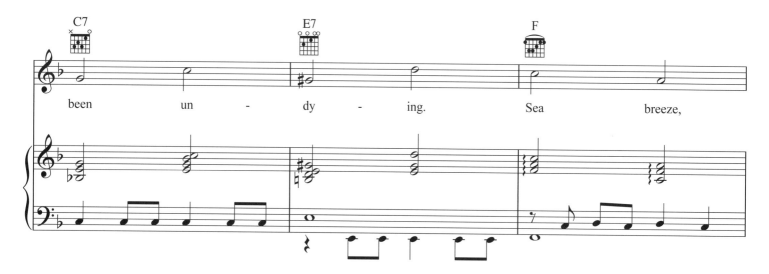

been un - dy - ing. Sea breeze,

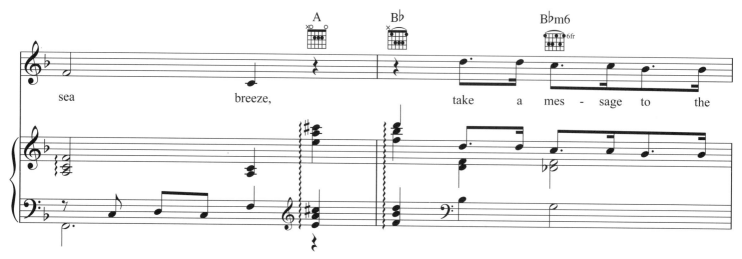

sea breeze, take a mes - sage to the

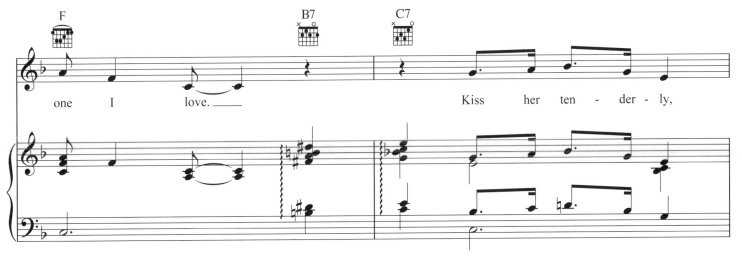

one I love. _____ Kiss her ten - der - ly,

tell her to wait for me, and say that I'll be com - ing

soon _____ to meet her by the blue la - goon.

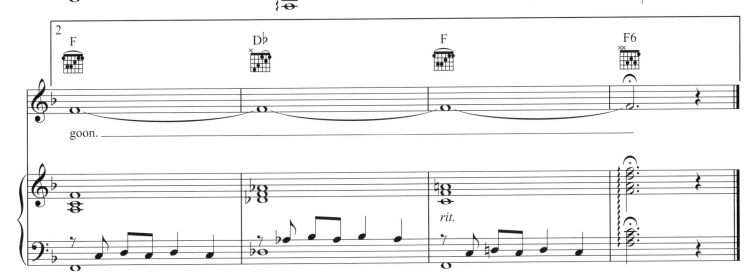

goon. _____

(Sittin' On)
THE DOCK OF THE BAY

Words and Music by STEVE CROPPER
and OTIS REDDING

watch'em roll a-way a - gain. ___ Yeah, ___ I'm sit - tin' on the dock of the bay, ___
noth-in's gon - na come my ___ way. ___ So ___ I'm just gon' sit on the dock of the bay, ___
make this dock my ___ home. ___ Now ___ I'm just gon' sit at the dock of the bay, ___

watch - in' the tide ___ roll ___ a - way. ___ Ooh, ___ I'm just

sit - tin' on the dock of the bay, ___ wast - in' time. ___

I ___

Looks like

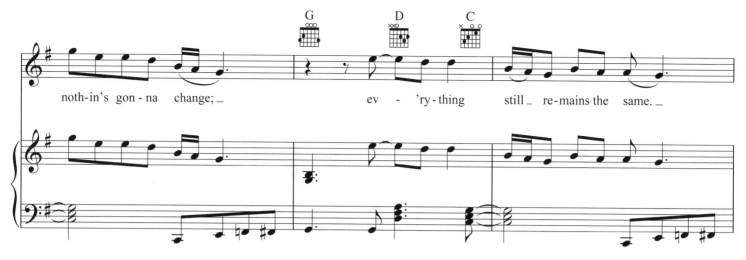

noth-in's gon-na change; ___ ev - 'ry-thing still ___ re-mains the same. ___

I can't do what ten peo-ple tell me ___ to do, ___ so I guess I'll re - main ___

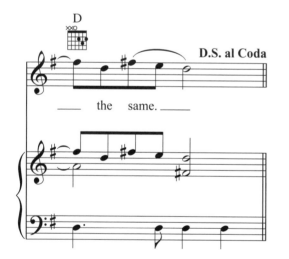

___ the same. ___

D.S. al Coda

CODA

Repeat and Fade

Optional Ending

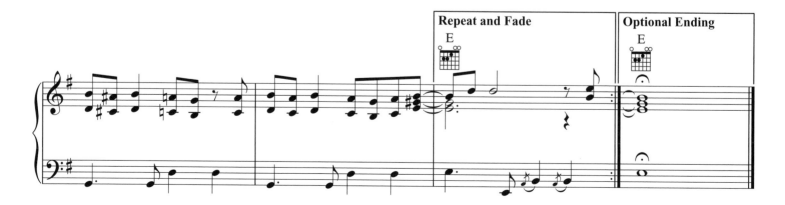

SLEEPY LAGOON

Words by JACK LAWRENCE
Music by ERIC COATES

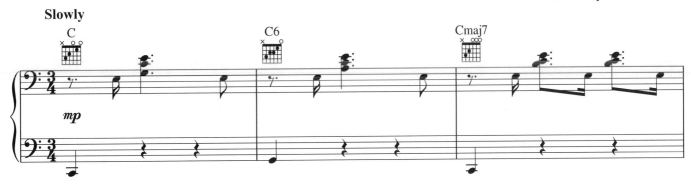

A sleep-y la - goon, a trop-i-cal moon, and two on an

is - land, _____ a sleep-y la - goon, and two hearts in

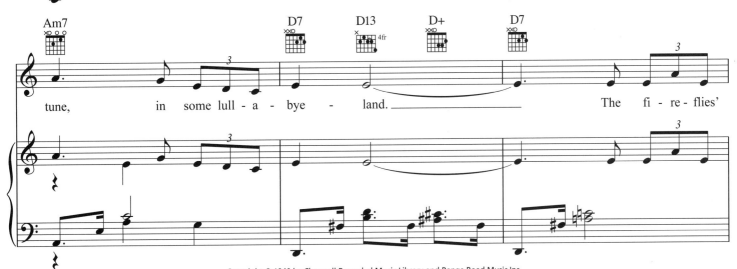

tune, in some lull-a-bye - land. _____ The fi-re-flies'

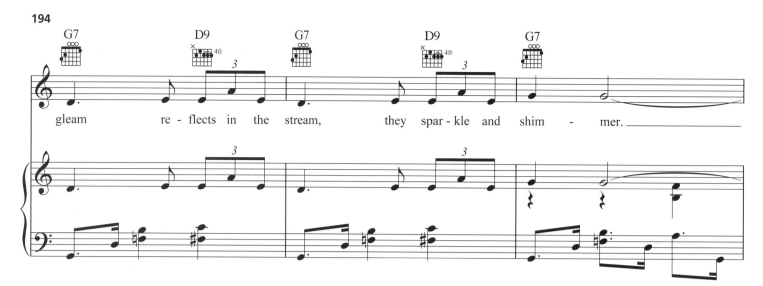

gleam re - flects in the stream, they spar - kle and shim - mer. _____

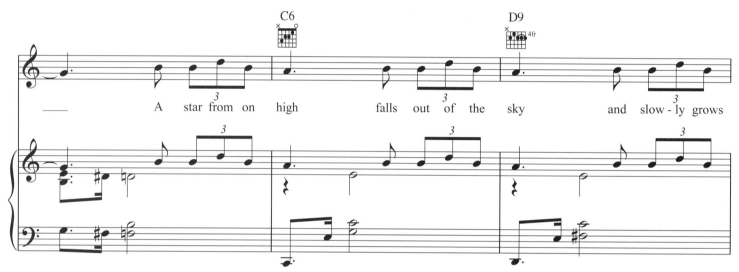

_____ A star from on high falls out of the sky and slow - ly grows

dim - mer. _____ The leaves from the trees all dance in the

breeze, and float on the rip - ples; _____ we're deep in a

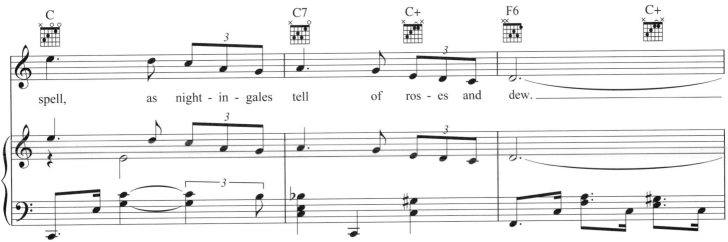

spell, as night - in - gales tell of ros - es and dew. ___

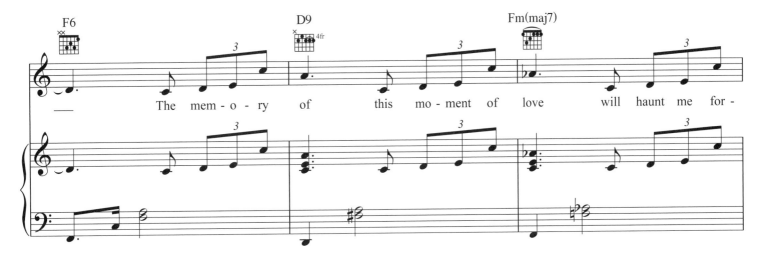

___ The mem - o - ry of this mo - ment of love will haunt me for -

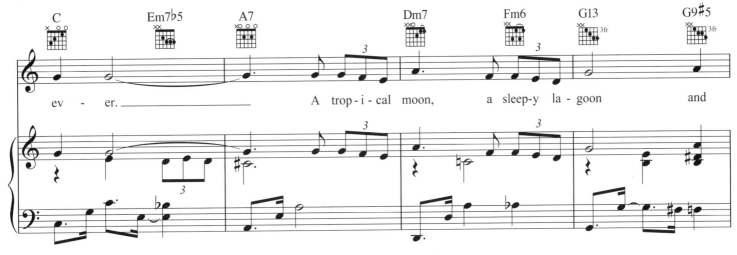

ev - er. ___ A trop - i - cal moon, a sleep - y la - goon and

you. A sleep - y la - you. ___

SONG OF THE ISLANDS

Words and Music by
CHARLES E. KING

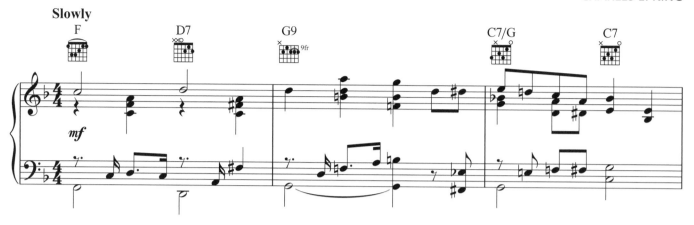

Ha - wai - i isles of beau - ty,_____ where skies are
Na - ni Ha - wa - i - i_____ ka mo - ku

blue and love is true,_____ where balm - y airs and gold - en
o Ke - a._____ Lei ha - a heo i ka le -

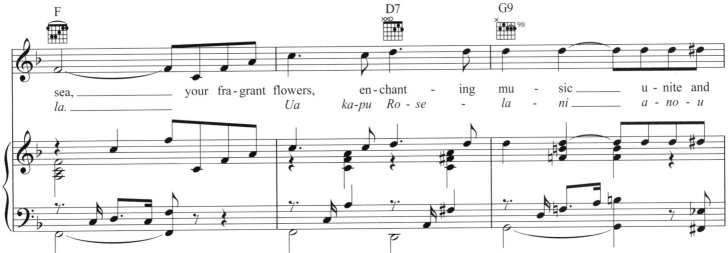

SUNDOWN

Words and Music by
GORDON LIGHTFOOT

Moderate Folk Rock

see her ly-in' back in her sat-in dress __ in a room where you do __ what you

don't __ con-fess. __ Sun-down, you bet-ter take care __ if I

Recorded a half step lower.

think it's a shame ___ when I get feel-in' bet-ter when I'm feel-in' no pain. ___
think it's a shame ___ when I get feel-in' bet-ter when I'm feel-in' no pain. ___

Some - times I think it's a shame ___ when I get feel-in' bet-ter when I'm
Sun - down, you bet-ter take care ___ if I find you been creep-in' 'round ___

To Coda

feel-in' no pain. ___
my back ___ stairs. ___ I can

pic - ture ev -'ry move that a man could make, ___ get-ting lost in her lov-ing is your

first __ mis - take. _____ Sun - down, you bet - ter take care __ if I

find you been creep - in' 'round __ my back stairs. __ Some - times I

think it's a sin __ when I feel like I'm win - nin' when I'm los - in' a - gain. __

Play 6 times

Guitar solo ad lib.

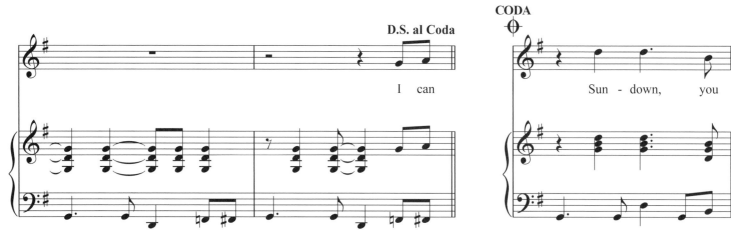

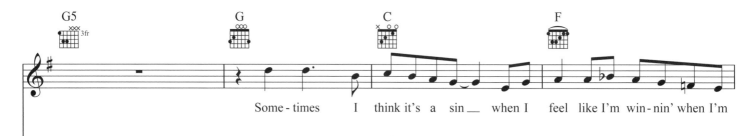

SUNNY DAYS, STARRY NIGHTS

Words and Music by
LEON POBER

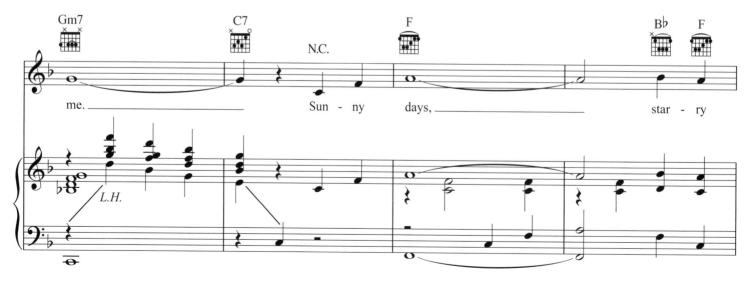

nights; _____ look a' that sky, _____ those won-der-ful

lights. _____ Star-ry nights, _____ sun-ny

days; _____ they make me love, love, love you in a mil-lion

ways.   Sun-ny ways. _____

8vb

SURF CITY

Words and Music by BRIAN WILSON
and JAN BERRY

Two girls __ for ev - 'ry boy! __

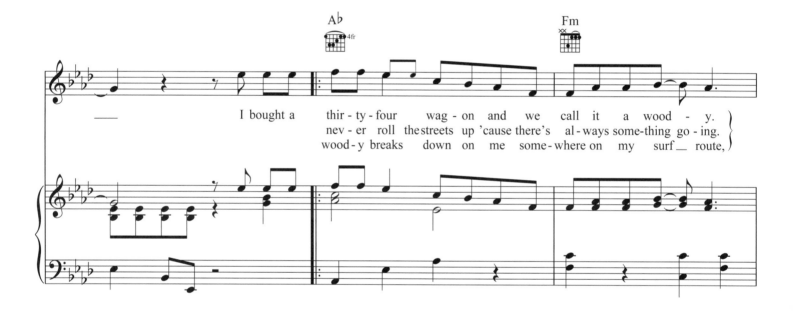

I bought a thir - ty - four wag - on and we call it a wood - y.
nev - er roll the streets up 'cause there's al - ways some - thing go - ing.
wood - y breaks down on me some - where on my surf __ route,

Surf Cit - y, here we come!
You know it's not ver - y cher - ry as an
They're ei - ther out surf - in' or they
I'll strap my board to my back and hitch a

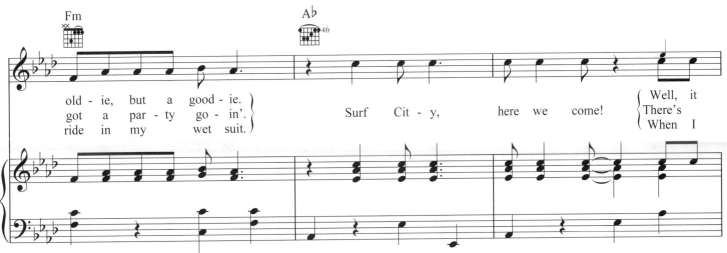

goin' to Surf Cit - y 'cause it's two to one. You know I'm goin' to Surf Cit - y, gon - na

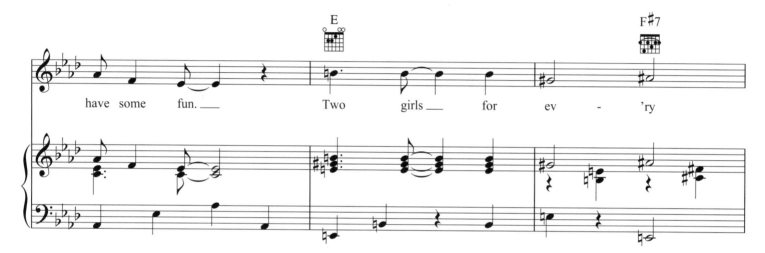

have some fun. ___ Two girls ___ for ev - 'ry

boy! ___

They say they two girls ___ for
And if my

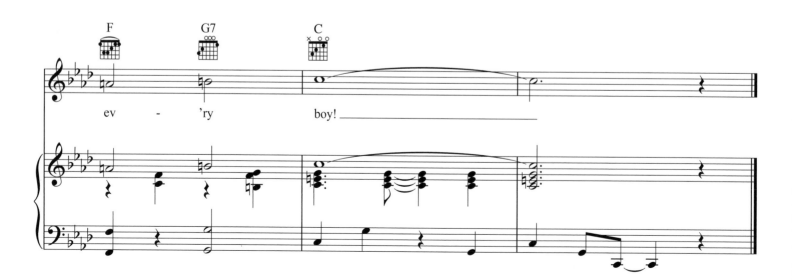

ev - 'ry boy! ___

SURFER GIRL

Words and Music by
BRIAN WILSON

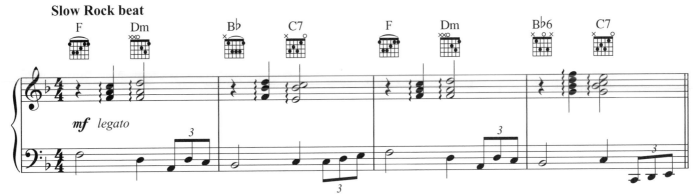

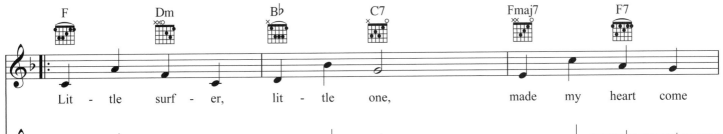

Lit - tle surf - er, lit - tle one, made my heart come

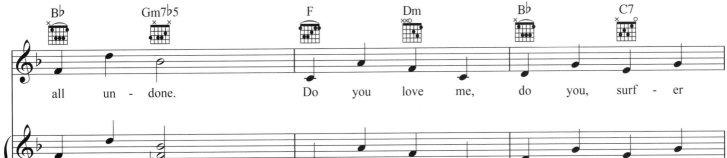

all un - done. Do you love me, do you, surf - er

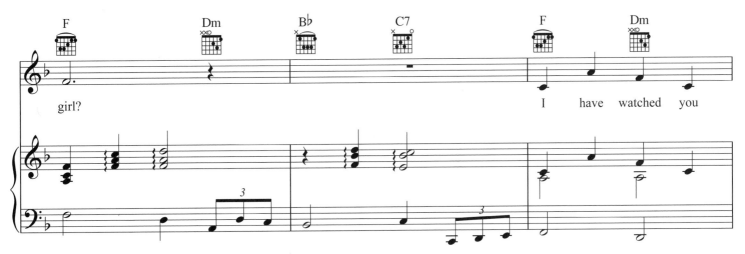

girl? I have watched you

on the shore, stand - ing by the o - cean's roar.

Do you love me, do you, surf - er girl?

We could ride the surf to - geth - er

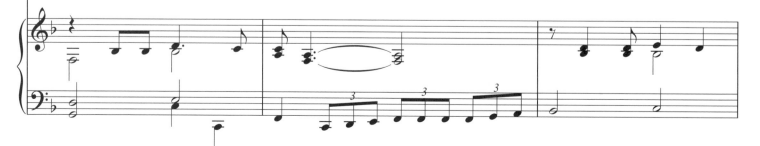

while our love would grow. _____ In my wood - y

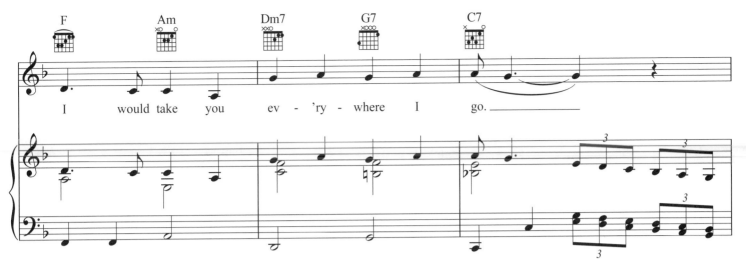

I would take you ev - 'ry - where I go. _____

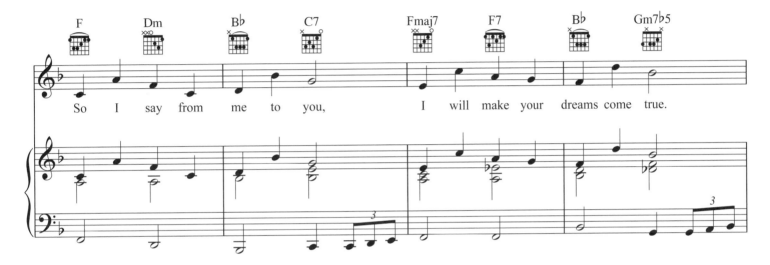

So I say from me to you, I will make your dreams come true.

Do you love me, do you, surf - er girl?

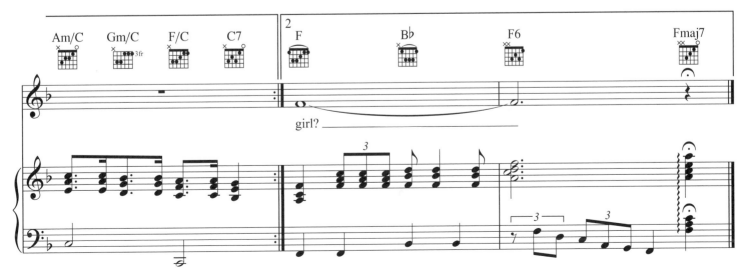

girl? _____

SURFIN' SAFARI

Words and Music by BRIAN WILSON
and MIKE LOVE

Bright Rock

Let's go surf-in' now, ev-'ry-bod-y's learn-in' how, come on a sa-fa-ri with me. _

Ear-ly in the morn-in' we'll be start-in' out, _ some they're
an-glin' in La-gu-na and Cerr-o A-zul, _ they're

hon-eys will be com-in' a - long. _ We're load-in' up our wood-y with the
kick-in' out in Do-hi-ni too. _ I tell you surf-in's run-nin' wild, it's get-tin'

boards in - side and head - in' out sing - in' our song.
big - ger ev - 'ry day from Ha - wai - i to the shores of Pe - ru.

Come on, ba - by, wait and see, __ yes, I'm gon - na take you surf - in' with me. __

Lone - some ba - by, wait and see, __ yes, I'm gon - na take you surf - in' with me. __

Let's go surf - in' now, ev - 'ry - bod - y's learn - in' how, come on a sa - fa - ri with me. __

SWEET SOMEONE

Words by GEORGE WAGGNER
Music by BARON KEYES

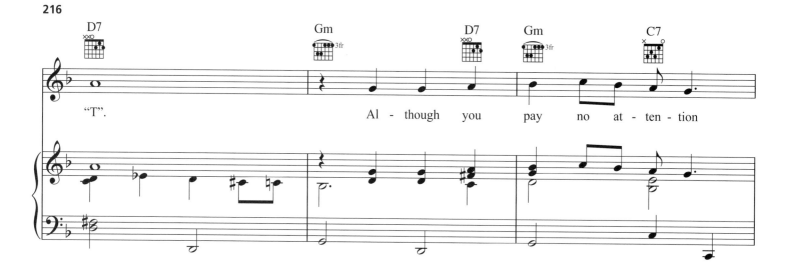

"T".   Al - though you pay no at - ten - tion

to me at all,   one kiss and,

need - less to men - tion,   I had to fall.

Now   I won - der   what's keep - ing us a -

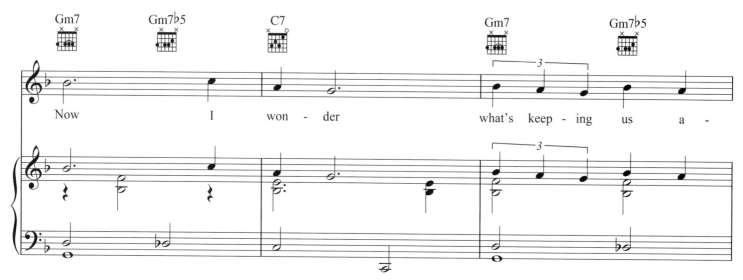

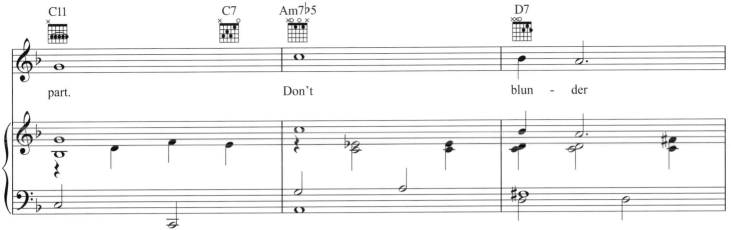

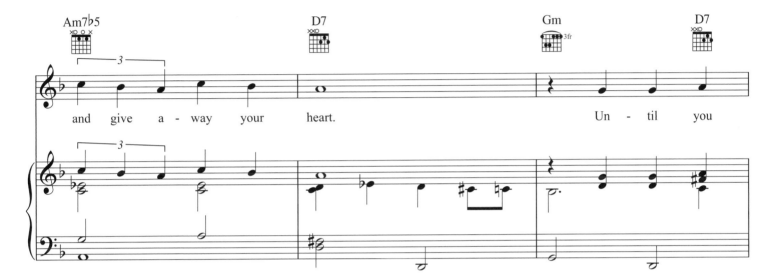

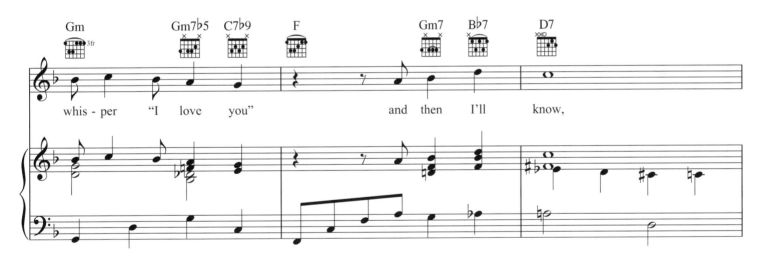

A TASTE OF HONEY

Words by RIC MARLOW
Music by BOBBY SCOTT

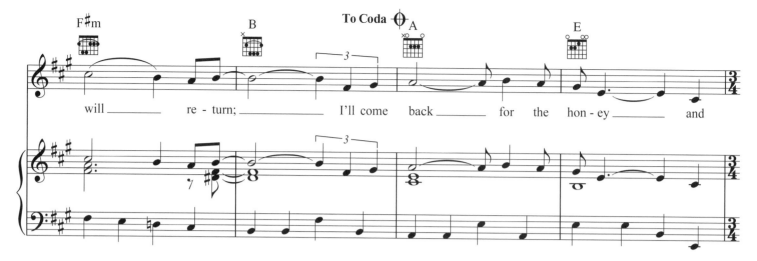

will _____ re - turn; _____ I'll come back _____ for the hon - ey _____ and

you. _____ (Doo dood - n' doo.)   (Doo dood - n' doo.)   Yours

D.S. al Coda

Slower

back _____ (he'll come back) _____ for _____ hon ey _____ (for the hon ey) _____ and

A tempo

you. _____

THREE LITTLE BIRDS

Words and Music by
BOB MARLEY

Moderately slow Reggae

"Don't

wor - ry   a - bout — a thing, —   'cause

ev - 'ry lit - tle thing   gon - na be al - right." —   Sing- in', "Don't

wor - ry   a - bout _ a   thing, __   'cause

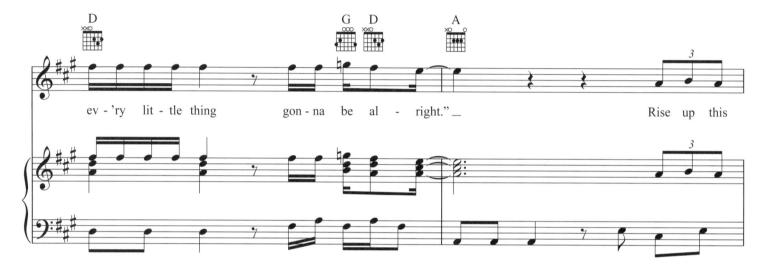

ev - 'ry lit - tle thing   gon - na be al - right." _   Rise up this

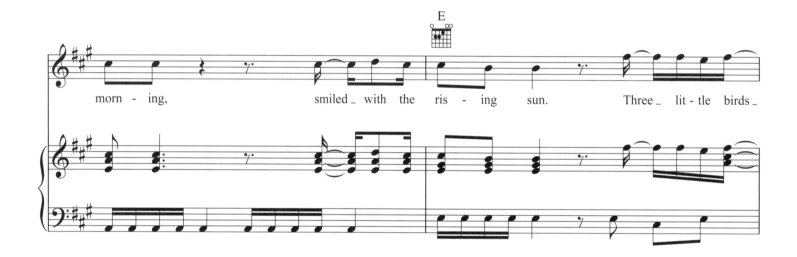

morn - ing,   smiled _ with the ris - ing sun.   Three _ lit - tle birds _

____   pitch by my door - step,   sing- in' sweet _

THE TIDE IS HIGH

Words and Music by JOHN HOLT,
TYRONE EVANS and HOWARD BARRETT

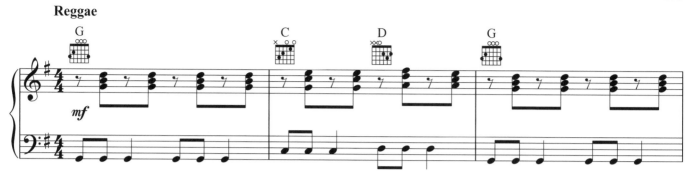

The tide is high, but I'm hold - ing on.

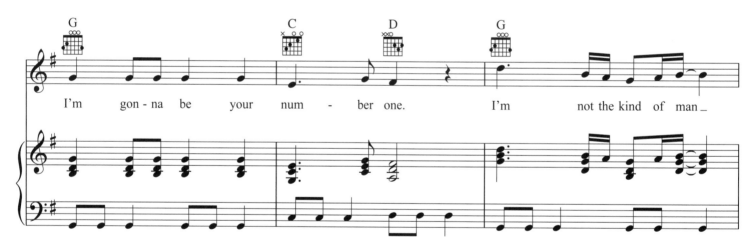

I'm gon - na be your num - ber one. I'm not the kind of man _

who gives up just _____ like that, _ no. _____ It's

not the things you do that real - ly hurts me bad,
Ev - ry man wants you to be his girl,

but it's the way you do the things you do to me.
but I'll wait, my dear, 'til it's my turn.

To Coda ⊕

I'm not the kind of man who gives up just like that,

no. The tide is high, but I'm hold - ing on.

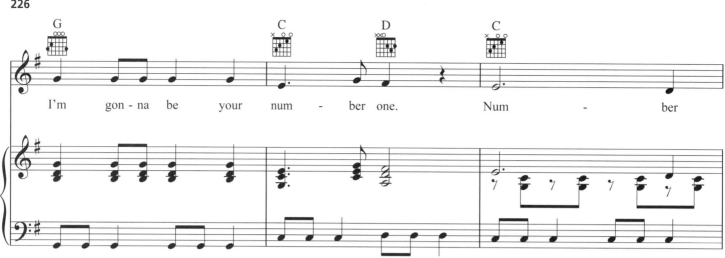

I'm gon - na be your num - ber one. Num - ber

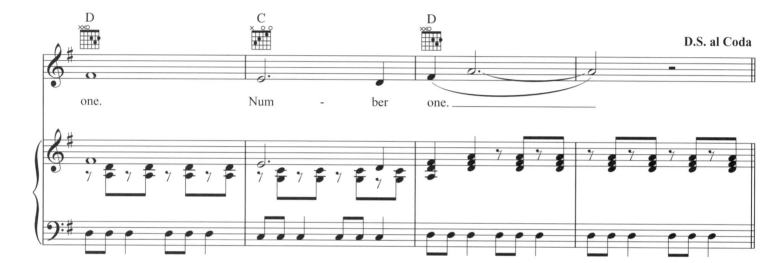

D.S. al Coda

one. Num - ber one. _____

CODA

no. _____   *Violin solo*

Ev - 'ry ___ man wants   you to

be his girl. But I'll wait, my dear, 'til it's my _____ turn.

I'm not the kind of man ___ who gives up just _____ like that, ___

no. _____ The tide is high, but I'm hold - ing on.

Repeat and Fade   **Optional Ending**

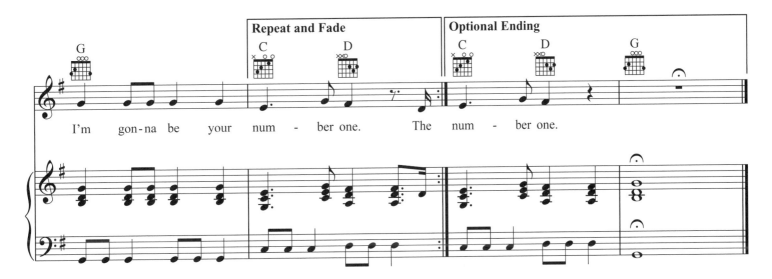

I'm gon-na be your num - ber one. The num - ber one.

TINY BUBBLES

Words and Music by
LEON POBER

with a feel-in' that I'm gon-na love you till the end of time.

So, here's to the gold-en moon, and here's to the sil-ver
So, here's to the gin-ger lei I give to you to-

sea; and most-ly, here's a toast to you and me.
day; and here's a kiss that will not fade a-way.

1
___ Ti - ny ___ Ti - ny

D.S. al Coda

CODA

time. ___

26 MILES
(Santa Catalina)

Words and Music by GLEN LARSON
and BRUCE BELLAND

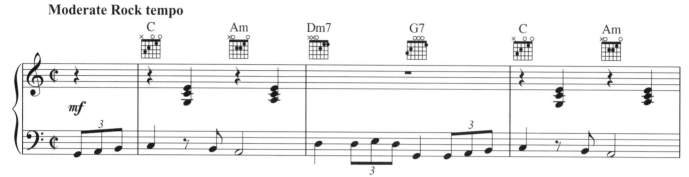

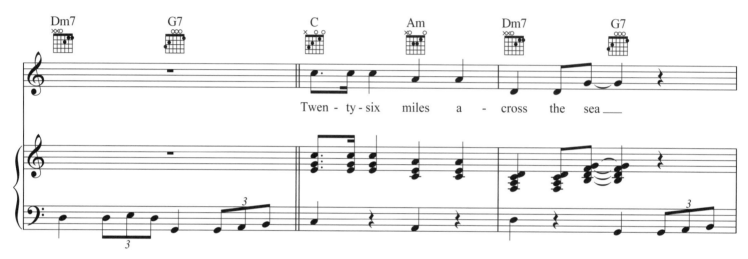

Twen-ty-six miles a-cross the sea ___

San - ta Ca - ta - li - na is a - wait - in' for me, ___ San - ta Ca - ta - li - na, the

is - land of ___ ro - mance, ___ ro - mance, ___ ro - mance, ___ ro - mance. ___

Wa - ter all a - round it ev - 'ry - where, ___ trop - i - cal trees and the

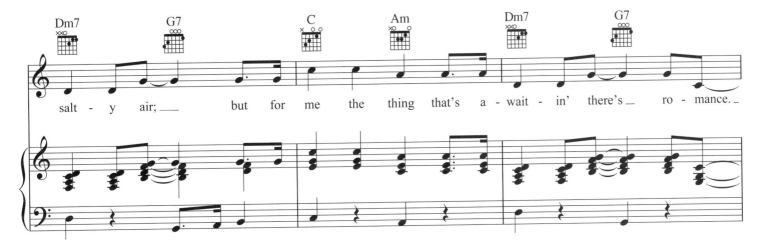

salt - y air; ___ but for me the thing that's a - wait - in' there's ___ ro - mance. ___

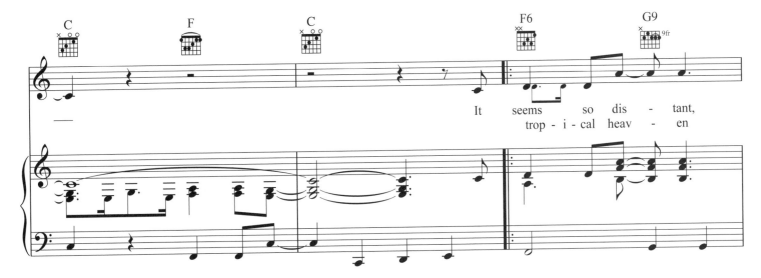

___ It seems so dis - tant, trop - i - cal heav - en

twen - ty - six miles ___ a - way, rest - in' in the wa - ter se - rene. ___ I'd
out in the o - cean cov - ered with ___ trees and girls. ___ If I

work for an - y - one, e - ven the Na - vy, who would
have to swim _____ I'd do it for - ev - er till I'm

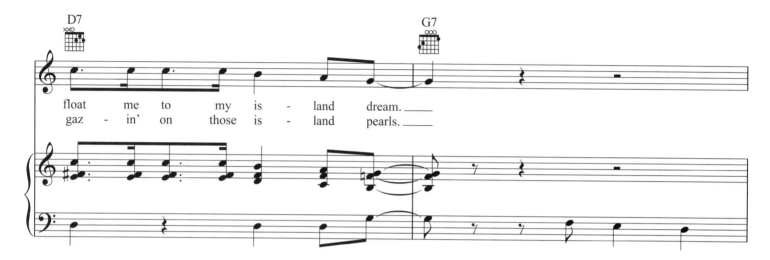

float me to my is - land dream. _____
gaz - in' on those is - land pearls. _____

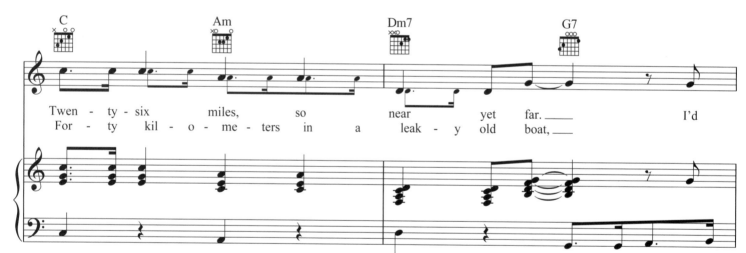

Twen - ty - six miles, so near yet far. _____ I'd
For - ty kil - o - me - ters in a leak - y old boat, _____

swim with just some wa - ter wings and my gui - tar. _____ I can leave the wings but I'll
an - y old _____ thing _____ that - 'll stay a - float. _____ When _____ we ar - rive we'll _____

need the gui-tar____ for ro-mance,____ ro-mance,____ ro-mance,____ ro-mance.____
all____ pro-mote_____ ro-mance,____ ro-mance,____ ro-mance,____

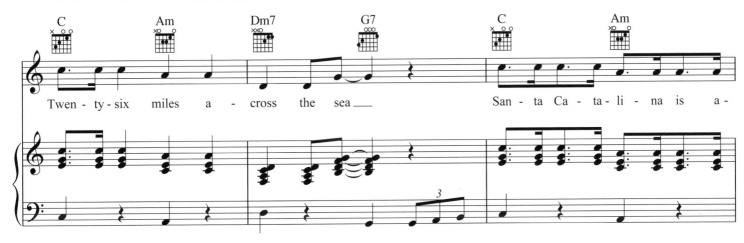

Twen-ty-six miles a-cross the sea____ San-ta Ca-ta-li-na is a-

wait-in' for me,____ San-ta Ca-ta-li-na, the is-land of____ ro-mance.____

____ A____ ro-mance.____

YELLOW BIRD

Words and Music by
IRVING BURGIE

Moderately, sweetly

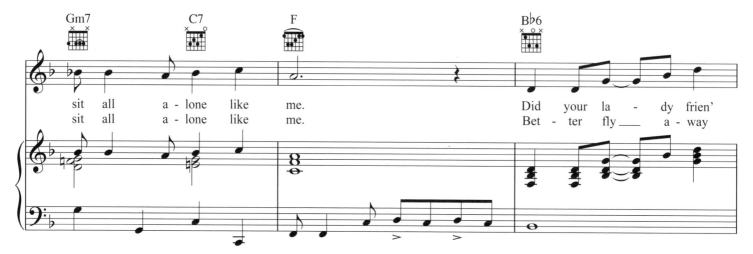

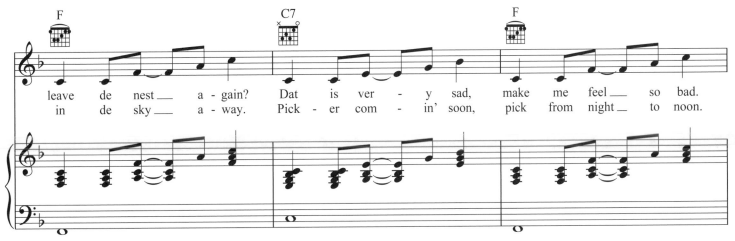

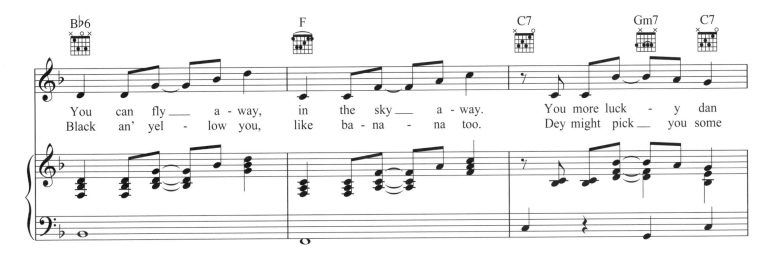

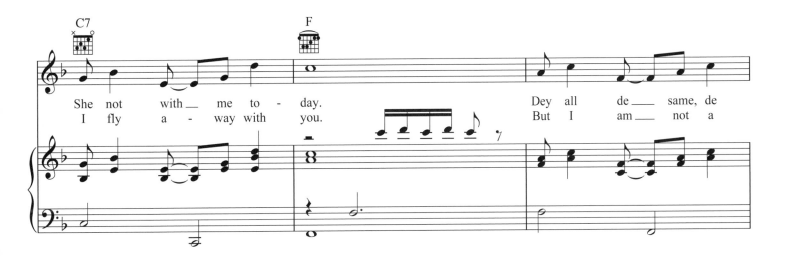

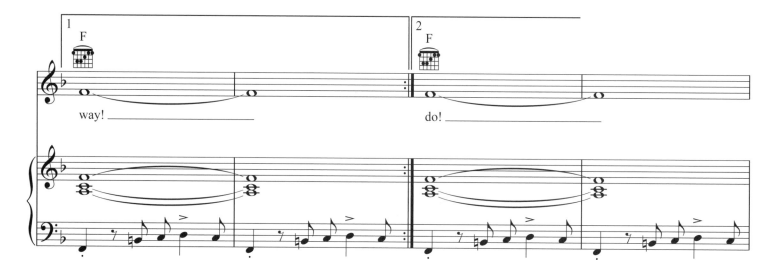

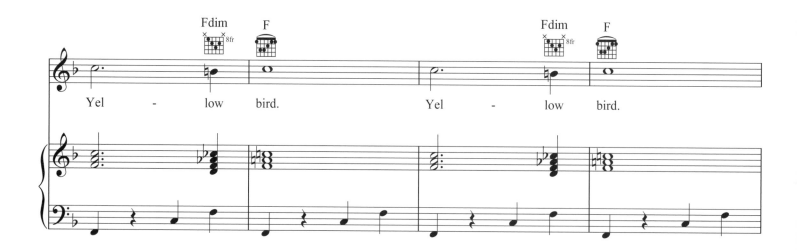

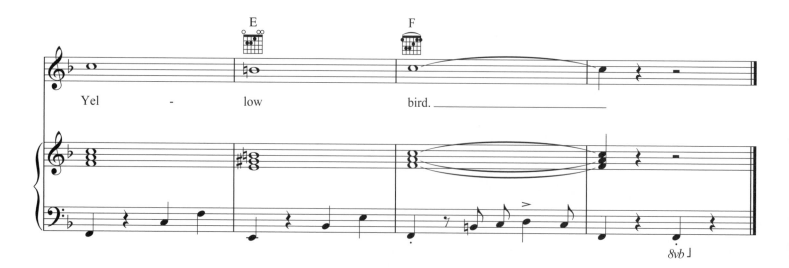

THE MOST REQUESTED SERIES

THE MOST REQUESTED ACOUSTIC SONGS

American Pie • Better Together • Black Water • The Boxer • Cat's in the Cradle • Crazy Little Thing Called Love • Free Fallin' • Friend of the Devil • I Walk the Line • I've Just Seen a Face • Landslide • More Than Words • Patience • Redemption Song • Summer Breeze • To Be with You • Toes • Wish You Were Here • and many more.
00001518 P/V/G $19.99

THE MOST REQUESTED BOSSA NOVA & SAMBA SONGS

Over 60 songs featuring that bossa nova and samba beat, including: Bonita • Don't Ever Go Away (Por Causa De Voce) • A Felicidade • The Girl from Ipanema (Garôta De Ipanema) • How Insensitive (Insensatez) • The Look of Love • Mas Que Nada • She's a Carioca • So Nice (Summer Samba) • Triste • and many more.
00154900 P/V/G $19.99

THE MOST REQUESTED BROADWAY SONGS

And I'm Telling You I'm Not Going • Aquarius • Can You Feel the Love Tonight • Corner of the Sky • Getting to Know You • Everything's Coming Up Roses • I Enjoy Being a Girl • It's Delovely • New York, New York • On My Own • Part of Your World • People • Seasons of Love • The Impossible Dream • Til There Was You • Tomorrow • What I Did for Love • and more.
00001557 P/V/G $19.99

THE MOST REQUESTED CHILDREN'S SONGS

A great collection of 75 songs perfect for children of all ages: Addams Family Theme • Be Our Guest • Edelweiss • Ghostbusters • Happy Birthday to You • Linus and Lucy • Put on a Happy Face • Sing • So Long, Farewell • Take Me Out to the Ball Game • This Land Is Your Land • You Are My Sunshine • and many more.
00145525 P/V/G $19.99

THE MOST REQUESTED CHRISTMAS SONGS

Blue Christmas • Christmas Time Is Here • Deck the Hall • Feliz Navidad • Grandma Got Run over by a Reindeer • Have Yourself a Merry Little Christmas • I'll Be Home for Christmas • Jingle Bells • Little Saint Nick • Nuttin' for Christmas • Rudolph the Red-Nosed Reindeer • Silent Night • Wonderful Christmastime • and more.
00001563 P/V/G $19.99

THE MOST REQUESTED CLASSIC ROCK SONGS

Africa • Bang a Gong (Get It On) • Don't Stop Believin' • Feelin' Alright • Hello, It's Me • Layla • The Letter • Life in the Fast Lane • Maybe I'm Amazed • Money • Only the Good Die Young • Peace of Mind • Small Town • Space Oddity • Tiny Dancer • Walk Away Renee • We Are the Champions • and more!
02501632 P/V/G $19.99

THE MOST REQUESTED COUNTRY SONGS

Cruise • Don't You Wanna Stay • Fly Over States • Gunpowder & Lead • How Do You Like Me Now?! • If I Die Young • Need You Now • Red Solo Cup • The Thunder Rolls • Wide Open Spaces • and more.
00127660 P/V/G $19.99

THE MOST REQUESTED COUNTRY LOVE SONGS

Always on My Mind • Amazed • Crazy • Forever and Ever, Amen • I Will Always Love You • Love Story • Stand by Your Man • Through the Years • When You Say Nothing at All • You're Still the One • and more.
00159649 P/V/G $19.99

THE MOST REQUESTED FOLK/POP SONGS

Blowin' in the Wind • City of New Orleans • Do You Believe in Magic • Fast Car • The House of the Rising Sun • If I Were a Carpenter • Leaving on a Jet Plane • Morning Has Broken • The Night They Drove Old Dixie Down • Puff the Magic Dragon • The Sound of Silence • Teach Your Children • and more.
00110225 P/V/G $19.99

THE MOST REQUESTED ISLAND SONGS

Beyond the Sea • Blue Hawaii • Coconut • Don't Worry, Be Happy • Electric Avenue • Escape (The Pina Colada Song) • I Can See Clearly Now • Island Girl • Kokomo • Redemption Song • Surfer Girl • Tiny Bubbles • and many more.
00197925 P/V/G $19.99

THE MOST REQUESTED JAZZ STANDARDS

All the Things You Are • Blue Skies • Embraceable You • Fascinating Rhythm • God Bless' the Child • I Got Rhythm • Mood Indigo • Pennies from Heaven • Satin Doll • Stella by Starlight • Summertime • The Very Thought of You • and more.
00102988 P/V/G $19.99

THE MOST REQUSTED MOVIE SONGS

Alfie • Born Free • Chariots of Fire • Endless Love • The Godfather (Love Theme) • Goldfinger • I Will Always Love You • James Bond Theme • Mrs. Robinson • Moon River • Over the Rainbow • The Rainbow Connection • The Rose • Stand by Me • Star Wars (Main Theme) • (I've Had) the Time of My Life • Tonight • The Wind Beneath My Wings • and more!
00102882 P/V/G $19.99

THE MOST REQUESTED PARTY SONGS

Another One Bites the Dust • Brown Eyed Girl • Celebration • Dancing Queen • Electric Slide • Get down Tonight • Girls Just Want to Have Fun • Hot Hot Hot • I Gotta Feeling • In Heaven There Is No Beer • Limbo Rock • The Loco-Motion • Shout • Twist and Shout • and many more.
00001576 P/V/G $19.99

THE MOST REQUESTED POP/FOLK SONGS

Alison • Annie's Song • Both Sides Now • The Boxer • California Girls • Fire and Rain • Joy to the World • Longer • Son-Of-A-Preacher Man • Summer in the City • Up on the Roof • and many more.
00145529 P/V/G $19.99

THE MOST REQUESTED WEDDING RECEPTION SONGS

Celebration • How Sweet It Is (To Be Loved by You) • Hungry Eyes • I Will Always Love You • In My Life • Isn't She Lovely • Last Dance • Let's Get It On • Love and Marriage • My Girl • Sunrise, Sunset • Unforgettable • The Way You Look Tonight • and more.
02501750 P/V/G $19.99

THE MOST REQUESTED HITS OF THE '60s

Aquarius • The Beat Goes On • Beyond the Sea • Happy Together • Hey Jude • King of the Road • Like a Rolling Stone • Save the Last Dance for Me • Son-Of-A-Preacher Man • These Eyes • Under the Boardwalk • Up on the Roof • and more.
00110207 P/V/G $19.99

THE MOST REQUESTED SONGS OF THE '70s

Bohemian Rhapsody • Desperado • Hello, It's Me • I Will Survive • Just the Way You Are • Let It Be • Night Moves • Rocky Mountain High • Summer Breeze • Time in a Bottle • You're So Vain • Your Song • and many more.
00119714 P/V/G $19.99

THE MOST REQUESTED SONGS OF THE '80s

Africa • Billie Jean • Come on Eileen • Every Breath You Take • Faith • Footloose • Hello • Here I Go Again • Jessie's Girl • Like a Virgin • Livin' on a Prayer • Open Arms • Rosanna • Sweet Child O' Mine • Take on Me • Uptown Girl • and more.
00111668 P/V/G $19.99

THE MOST REQUESTED SONGS OF THE '90s

All I Wanna Do • ...Baby One More Time • Barely Breathing • Creep • Fields of Gold • From a Distance • Livin' La Vida Loca • Losing My Religion • Semi-Charmed Life • Smells like Teen Spirit • 3 AM • Under the Bridge • Who Will Save Your Soul • You Oughta Know • and more.
00111971 P/V/G $19.99

BIG BOOKS of Music

Our "Big Books" feature big selections of popular titles under one cover, perfect for performing musicians, music aficionados or the serious hobbyist. All books are arranged for piano, voice, and guitar, and feature stay-open binding, so the books lie flat without breaking the spine.

BIG BOOK OF BALLADS – 2ND ED.
62 songs.
00310485 .... $19.95

BIG BOOK OF BIG BAND HITS
84 songs.
00310701 .... $22.99

BIG BOOK OF BLUEGRASS SONGS
70 songs.
00311484 .... $19.95

BIG BOOK OF BLUES
80 songs.
00311843 .... $19.99

BIG BOOK OF BROADWAY
70 songs.
00311658 .... $19.95

BIG BOOK OF CHILDREN'S SONGS
55 songs.
00359261 .... $16.99

GREAT BIG BOOK OF CHILDREN'S SONGS
76 songs.
00310002 .... $15.99

FANTASTIC BIG BOOK OF CHILDREN'S SONGS
66 songs.
00311062 .... $17.95

BIG BOOK OF CHRISTMAS SONGS – 2ND ED.
126 songs.
00311520 .... $19.95

BIG BOOK OF CLASSICAL MUSIC
100 songs.
00310508 .... $19.99

BIG BOOK OF CONTEMPORARY CHRISTIAN FAVORITES – 3RD ED.
50 songs.
00312067 .... $21.99

BIG BOOK OF '50s & '60s SWINGING SONGS
67 songs.
00310982 .... $19.95

BIG BOOK OF FOLKSONGS
125 songs.
00312549 .... $19.99

BIG BOOK OF FRENCH SONGS
70 songs.
00311154 .... $19.95

BIG BOOK OF GERMAN SONGS
78 songs.
00311816 .... $19.99

BIG BOOK OF GOSPEL SONGS
100 songs.
00310604 .... $19.95

BIG BOOK OF HYMNS
125 hymns.
00310510 .... $17.95

BIG BOOK OF IRISH SONGS
76 songs.
00310981 .... $19.95

BIG BOOK OF ITALIAN FAVORITES
80 songs.
00311185 .... $19.99

BIG BOOK OF JAZZ – 2ND ED.
75 songs.
00311557 .... $19.95

BIG BOOK OF LATIN AMERICAN SONGS
89 songs.
00311562 .... $19.95

BIG BOOK OF LOVE SONGS
80 songs.
00310784 .... $19.95

BIG BOOK OF MOTOWN
84 songs.
00311061 .... $19.95

BIG BOOK OF MOVIE MUSIC
72 songs.
00311582 .... $19.95

BIG BOOK OF NOSTALGIA
158 songs.
00310004 .... $24.99

BIG BOOK OF OLDIES
73 songs.
00310756 .... $19.95

THE BIG BOOK OF PRAISE & WORSHIP
52 songs.
00140795 .... $22.99

BIG BOOK OF RAGTIME PIANO
63 songs.
00311749 .... $19.95

BIG BOOK OF ROCK
78 songs.
00311566 .... $22.95

BIG BOOK OF SOUL
71 songs.
00310771 .... $19.95

BIG BOOK OF STANDARDS
86 songs.
00311667 .... $19.95

BIG BOOK OF SWING
84 songs.
00310359 .... $19.95

BIG BOOK OF TORCH SONGS – 2ND ED.
75 songs.
00310561 .... $19.99

BIG BOOK OF TV THEME SONGS
78 songs.
00310504 .... $19.95

BIG BOOK OF WEDDING MUSIC
77 songs.
00311567 .... $19.95

HAL•LEONARD®

Prices, contents, and availability subject to change without notice.

Visit **www.halleonard.com**
for our entire catalog and to view our complete songlists.

0916